THE WIND BLOWS TO THE EAST

STEPHAN A. DZEROVYCH

authorHOUSE™

1663 LIBERTY DRIVE, SUITE 200
BLOOMINGTON, INDIANA 47403
(800) 839-8640
WWW.AUTHORHOUSE.COM

First published by AuthorHouse 07/18/05

ISBN: 1-4208-6125-5 (e)
ISBN: 1-4208-6123-9 (sc)

Library of Congress Control Number: 2005904943

Printed in the United States of America
Bloomington, Indiana

This book is printed on acid-free paper.

National Flags obtained from www.theodora.com

FOREWORD

The intent of this book is to stimulate the reader's thoughts on important current and future issues facing the world. Whether the reader agrees or disagrees with the author's projections is of little importance.

TABLE OF CONTENTS

Introduction   1

Current Status   16
    West   19
      United States   19
      Western-Oriented Europe (EU) 31
      Canada   35
      Turkey   36

    East   37
      China   37
      Japan   42
      India   46
      Indonesia   48
      Other Eastern Countries   49

    East/West Links   49
      Russia   50
      Islamic Belt   58

Hard Going in the West   63

East on the March   73

Future Developments (Beyond 2005)   82
    Near Term (2006-2025)   83
      West   83
      East   88
    Long-Term (2026-2100)   90

Sources   95

INTRODUCTION

The world never rests. Progressive changes shape new generations with the rate of progress in close synchronization with the world's numerical, cultural, intellectual, emotional, and economic growth. History shows that population growth, under the right conditions, stimulates progress or the advancement toward a higher stage of development. Conversely population decrease brings about regression.

Population growth creates a demand for goods, which prompts the development of the industry and infrastructure needed to produce them. A concentration of labor then leads to urbanization. Also, a military force is typically developed which serves the purpose of protecting or, if deemed profitable, expanding the acquired wealth. Population decrease has the opposite effect, which causes the industrial production, infrastructure, and need for militarism to decline.

As populations grow, the level of progress is directly related to the state of tranquility during the period and the characteristics of the population mix. Either wars or internal, ethnic, religious, or class, conflicts can obstruct progress. Populations with low literacy rates and high percentages of people who are unable to be part of the workforce (for example, the elderly and handicapped) also have a negative effect on the degree of progress.

For most of written history, which began about 4000 BC, the Greater Near East (Middle and Near East) and the Far East were the most important regions from which new ideas and inventions fueled the progress of world civilization. One of the most significant inventions from the Greater Near East was the art of writing, which facilitated the transfer of these ideas from East to West.

During the past 500 years, however, beginning with the high point of the Renaissance around 1500 AD, Western civilizations began to make vast progress while Eastern civilizations started to lag. The demand for goods by a spirited, progressive, and rapidly growing population in the West fueled the Industrial Revolution. Nations of Western Europe, and later North America, experienced strong economic growth, which resulted in accumulation of wealth. Gradually, ideas and information started to flow from West to East, reversing the trend of earlier times.

By 1900, most of the technical skills and economic power were vested in the relatively wealthy developed nations of the West. The nations of the East, which once spearheaded the progress of the world's civilization, now became known as the "developing nations" of the world, a designation of lesser economic, social, and political development than their counterparts in the West.

Today, despite regional conflicts, threats of wide-scale wars, and the menace of terrorism, mankind is making more efficient use of the world than any generation in the past, largely due to this extraordinary period of Western preeminence. The monumental achievements of this period, however, overshadow subtle, but far-reaching, changes that are gradually beginning to take place, which will blow the winds of progress back in the easterly direction and shape the world's generations to come.

The West is gradually losing momentum as the population growth rate of its countries is slowing and in some cases even declining. The optimistic and progressive outlook of Western people slowly diminishes as the percentage of older people in their population increases. The sixty-five year and older, or senior, age group already exceeds 10 percent in all of the major Western countries. It is expected that this percentage will continue to increase sharply. Estimates are that by 2025, about 20 percent of the population will be seniors, with that percentage increasing to roughly 25 percent by 2050. Over time, economic growth will slow as demand for goods gradually declines and the financial burden of providing healthcare for a much larger segment of the population increases. Wars against terrorism will further drain the economic resources of the United States and its Western allies. The spirit of the Western populations will lack the initiative and vigor of the past. The greatest impact, initially, will be on the nations of Europe. However, the U.S. will also be severely affected as the economic advantage gradually shifts to the populous, initially technologically inferior but more enthusiastic and dynamic, developing nations of the East. Additionally, these populations continue to grow at a robust pace while maintaining a roughly 50 percent lower 65+ age group than the West. First China, then, India, will be in the forefront as they experience their own Eastern brand of the Renaissance. South Korea and Japan, already technologically advanced with the assistance of the West, will shed their current Western orientation and gradually join them to form a formidable and wealthy East Asian economic block, which, by 2050, will comprise about half of the world's population.

Looking back on history, population growth began slowly. Small communities, which existed in the early days of civilization, did not have the critical mass of people needed to organize on a large scale. A formal structure was not necessary, as the small groups of people could provide for their own needs. Thus, the ingredients essential for rapid cultural progress and population growth were absent.

Development of larger and more organized population centers in the Greater Near East and the Far East, like Ur in Mesopotamia around 3000 BC, Memphis in ancient Egypt around 3100 BC, Harappa in the Indus Valley around 2500 BC, and Anyang along the Huang He River in China around 1500 BC immensively advanced the rate of progress of the cultural, economic, and political development of the world's civilization. From these areas, civilized ways of life and knowledge spread through commerce, conquest, and migration to other regions of the world including Athens (450 BC), Rome (100 BC), and later, Western Europe.

From about 1000 BC until about 1500 AD, the world's population grew at a relatively modest pace from about 50 million to nearly 500 million at an average growth rate of about 18 million people per 100 years. The world's population growth rate dropped noticeably below the average during the regressive years of the Middle Ages (450 AD – 900 AD), also known as the Dark Ages in Western European history, and experienced large, substantially above average growth spurts both during the Golden Age of Athens (461 BC – 431 BC) and following the end of the Dark Ages beginning with the period referred to as the High Middle Ages (1000 AD – 1200 AD), showing a clear correlation between people's positive outlook, population growth, and progress.

At the same time as the Western European civilization struggled through the Middle Ages, civilized cultures were prospering in the East. In India, a great civilization flourished under the Gupta Dynasty. In Southeastern Europe, the Byzantine Empire enjoyed great wealth and in the Greater Near East, the Moslem Empire reached enormous power. The Moslems established a new religion, Islam, and converted millions of people. Many ideas and inventions of the Moslems were brought back to Europe by the Crusaders. China's civilization also reached new heights of achievement and Japan enjoyed its Golden Age. Many of their ideas and inventions found their way into Western civilization as well.

In the early 1300's, a 300-year period of cultural awakening, called the Renaissance, started in Western Europe. Artists and scholars endorsed the idea of individual freedom and urged people to relinquish the ancient customs and rules that governed life during the Middle Ages. The Renaissance, from about 1300 AD to 1600 AD, was a period of enthusiasm, great literature, and art. Numerous inventions were also created during this period. Columbus sailed his historic voyage to America, one of many to be undertaken by explorers. Trade and commerce expanded rapidly which raised the European standard of living and led to the establishment of European colonies overseas. It was during the early part of this exuberant period, around 1450 AD, that the world experienced a very sharp and sustained rise in the population growth rate on the order of 100 million people per 100 years. The rate continued to accelerate until the 1960's, except during the period of the bubonic plague in Europe in the 1600's. It was indeed this extended spurt in population growth that generated the demand for goods and services in the early 1700's, which led to the Industrial Revolution. Goods, up until then, had been produced mostly by hand at home and in small workshops. However, these methods were not sufficient enough to supply a fast-growing population. Production of goods could be done more effectively in factories by machinery. Initially started in England, the Industrial Revolution spread throughout Europe and then, later, to the United States. The mood of the world's Western populations was optimistic, spirited, enterprising, and adventurous, despite the many social evils brought on by the Industrial Revolution which included poor working standards, child labor, city slums, and environmental pollution. Large cities grew rapidly, as people left rural areas to find work in the cities. The expansion of colonialism satisfied the need for raw materials and provided markets for goods produced. Growing wealth and technology were brought together to satisfy the increasing demands of the marketplace. This economic boom in the West only marginally extended to the East. Some knowledge was transferred from West to East, but the technical skills and wealth remained in the West.

The Industrial Revolution brought on changes that were undoubtedly the result of long, gradual, and evolutionary development. However, the precipitating factor was the increased population growth period in Europe, starting around 1450 AD, which finally produced the critical mass of people needed to rapidly accelerate the rate of progress. Advancements in technology, sanitation, medicine, and means of food distribution made a significant drop in the death rate possible, further accelerating the population growth rate.

In the next 250 years, between 1700 and 1950, the world's population more than quadrupled to about 2.5 billion people. This set the stage for an even greater leap forward to 6 billion people by the year 2000. Cultural, economic, and political changes came quickly as man multiplied rapidly and began to use the earth's resources and new technologies fully. With the West leading the way, progress proceeded on all fronts. During the period between 1700 and 2000, man developed, among others, the spinning jenny, the steam engine, the electric bulb, the telephone, the automobile, the airplane, the transistor, the computer, the atomic power, the missile, and the spacecraft to take him to the moon.

Concurrently, changes in population composition began to take place. The opportunity for better life in the wealthy nations of the West, including U.S., Canada, and Western Europe, attracted immigrants from countries in other parts of the world. The U.S. in particular had a continuing large influx of immigrants, first from Europe and then from Latin America and Asia. Today, about 14.5 percent of the U.S. population is Hispanic and 4.5 percent is Asian. The two ethnic groups are the fastest growing population segments and, in the course of time, will fully change the fabric of the U.S. population. By 2100, Hispanics will comprise more than a third of the U.S. population. Other countries will also experience changes in their population distributions due to different growth rates among their ethnic and religious populations. By 2050, about 15 percent of France's population will be Moslem and 30 percent of Israel's population will be Israeli Arabs. By 2100, over half of Israel's population will be ethnic Arabs.

Throughout history, the ruling, wealthier, or the culturally more advanced group, even if it represented a smaller percentage of the population, generally assumed control of the country, often with dire consequences for the majority. In modern, democratic times, however, the majority will prevail over the minority elite and thus modify the fabric of that society to largely reflect their cultural traditions or religious beliefs. Hence, the U.S., France, Israel, and other countries as well, will likely have an entirely different cultural, social, and political character in the future than they do today.

Another significant demographic manifestation of modern times is the changing age distribution of the world's population. In the developed world, the 0-19 youth age group is declining rapidly, as fertility rates are dropping sharply. By the year 2050, this age group in most of the industrialized West will represent on the average only 20 percent of the total population, roughly a 25 percent drop from current levels. Much of the vitality present in young populations will be lost. By 2010, the 20-64 working age group will have peaked around 60 percent in most of the West, followed by a gradual decline to about only 52 percent in the 2040 to 2050 time frame, before steadying at that level. About 8 percent of the highest spending core consumer base will be the lost in the West. Western corporations, including those in the U.S., will turn increasingly to outsourcing jobs to lesser developed countries in Asia, South America, and later even Africa to make up for the 8 percent drop in the workforce. Retirement at the age of seventy, or even older, may become the norm. The most dramatic change, however, will occur in the 65+ senior age group. As medical advances allow people to live longer lives, the 65+ age group will become the fastest growing population segment in the developed countries of the world. In most nations, it will be the only growing segment. The Americans, Canadians, and the Western Europeans in this age group will average roughly 25 percent by the year 2050, or almost double the current average level of 15 percent. The percentage of the population reporting long-term illness or disability increases sharply from age 65. In the U.S., 45 percent of the population in the 65+ age group shows some level of disability; 25 percent has difficulty going outside the home. The state of health of the rapidly increasing elderly population segment will have a negative affect on the mood of the population as a whole. As the larger aged population further dampens the energy and spirit of the West, their governments will have to contend with enormous economic burdens to provide pension and healthcare benefits for them. The demographic spread of the next 50 years will represent an increasingly less enterprising, more frugal consumer base, which, at best, will translate into lower productivity and economic growth, and, at worst, into an economic downturn. If Japan, which already has reached the 20 percent level in the 65+ age group, is used as an indicator, a prolonged period of economic stagnation could be in order for the West.

Most of the developing world, with the exception of sub-Saharan Africa, is 30 to 50 years behind the West in experiencing similar demographic changes. While sub-Saharan Africa is about 50 to 75 years behind the West.

The majority of the developing nations in the East, as opposed to the West, still have very young populations. The 0-19 youth age group makes up 30 to 50 percent of their populations. The large percentage of young people in the demographic spread represents an unstable and volatile population segment, particularly in a high unemployment scenario. When members of this group mature and begin to enter the workforce, lack of jobs creates a breeding ground for militants. Much of the unrest and terrorism in the Islamic world can be attributed to this explosive environment. The Unites States experienced, to a much lesser degree, a similar situation in the 1960's when the baby boom years following the end of World War II swelled the 0-19 youth age group to 38 percent. As the economy passed through a prolonged recession, deadly riots broke out in the black ghettos of Watts (Los Angeles) in 1965.

Although the world's rate of population growth has slowed since 1963 because of lower fertility, particularly in the developed nations, the world's population growth continues and will do so into the second half of the century, albeit at a reduced growth rate. Today's population, which numbers 6.4 billion, will reach 9.2 billion in 2050 and 10 billion in 2075. Most of the growth will come from the developing nations of the world; U.S. population will grow modestly and Europe will experience a decline. Gradually, smaller or slower growing, as well as aging populations in the West, will dampen the demand for goods, which will, in turn, create overcapacity and lead to severe economic and social problems. A period of industrial stagnation will encompass the West, particularly Western Europe, through the middle part of the 21st century and possibly beyond. The unity of the West itself will be under pressure due to political, social, and economic differences. The West's economic boom will gradually shift to the East where a belated Industrial Revolution, first started in Japan in the 1950's, will continue conservatively through most of the 21st century and include many of the nations of East Asia. Population growth will keep pace with the economic expansion. By 2050, about three-fifths of the world's population will be in Asia. China will emerge as the main catalyst of the Asian boom, replacing Japan, whose stagnated economy already struggles with an aging and shrinking population. Over time, India, Indonesia, Malaysia, Thailand, and other Asian countries, whose economies are currently expanding, will begin to fully participate in the economic prosperity. Japan and South Korea, two countries with an existing strong industrial base, will experience a strengthening of their economies as they join the others in the East's revival.

In China, the economic expansion, driven by investment, domestic consumption, and overseas demand for its goods, is already well underway. Development of a modern infrastructure that is capable of maintaining the expansion has begun with the construction of extensive road, rail, water, and power networks. As China's population grows to 1.5 billion people by 2035, rural agricultural workers will move into cities creating some of the largest population centers in the world. Reminiscent of the beginning of the Industrial Revolution in Europe, hardships will accompany the process. Unsanitary working conditions, child labor, and pollution are already common in China. In due time, however, the industrial expansion will produce a hard working, disciplined, vibrant, and efficient workforce which will fuel further progress and accumulation of wealth, similarly to how the Industrial Revolution affected the West.

Much of the rest of the world will be watching from the sidelines as the winds of progress shift from West to East. Russia, straddling both the East and the West, will benefit economically from the Asian economic expansion through increased trade, as well as politically by acting as a link between the East and the West. However, Russia's population is both aging and declining rapidly and, by 2050, will dwindle down to 110 million people, a third of which will be in the 65+ age group. Under these circumstances, it will be difficult for Russia to fully revive its industrial base. Nonetheless, Russia's rich natural resources, particularly oil and gas, will keep its economy growing. Russia has recovered well from the breakup of the Soviet Union and will continue to be a major power in the world.

The Islamic Belt (I-Belt) countries, which stretch from the Northwest tip of Africa through the Greater Near East into Asia, have population growth rates that exceed those of both the West and the East. They also have the largest oil reserves in the world and will continue to be the world's major supplier of oil. Nonetheless, their very youthful populations, on the average 40 percent in the 0-19 age group, low literacy rates, only in the 50-75 percent range, and authoritarian governments create an unstable, often militant environment, which is not conducive to industrial development. Rivalries among Islamic sects and governments prevent a unified front. Those circumstances are often exploited by other countries. Externally, they are also subject to political and military pressures from the West, particularly the U.S., who is eager to have full access to their oil reserves to satisfy its national interest. Conflicts develop when extremist groups or unfriendly governments threaten the oil supplies that are vital to the Western economies.

South America, whose population growth will not begin to slow until later in the first half of the 21st century, has the potential to experience its own economic revival. However, it is somewhat removed from the rest of the world and, at least currently, it is too heavily dependent on the U.S. economy to fully realize its potential. Large internal and external debts are also negative factors. Nonetheless, Brazil and Mexico have the essentials, which include large and growing populations as well as rich natural resources, to become the leaders in a South American economic and political block that could start to challenge the U.S. dominance of the Western Hemisphere around the second half of this century.

By about 2075, it will become increasingly apparent that the grandeur of the world has returned to its original birthplace in the East. Also around this time, the world's population growth will begin to stabilize as the populations of new developing nations, especially those in Asia and Africa, gradually begin to experience a decline in fertility rates. Most countries will have predominantly aging populations. Industrial retrenchment or the reduction in industrial capacity, which will begin in Europe about 2025, will spread gradually to most of the world in varying degrees of severity, reaching a peak around 2075, when the world's population growth is projected to begin its decline. A phenomenon, almost the opposite of what occurred during the Industrial Revolution, will face most of the world in about 70 years, with difficult social, economic, and political problems to resolve. As the world struggles to regain economic balance, both the East and West, out of necessity for their own well-being and respect for humanity, will join forces to overcome the damaging consequences of the world's industrial retrenchment and start to steer the world back on a stable course.

The world population growth from 1700 to 2100 is shown in Figure 1.

FIGURE 1: HISTORICAL POPULATION GROWTH

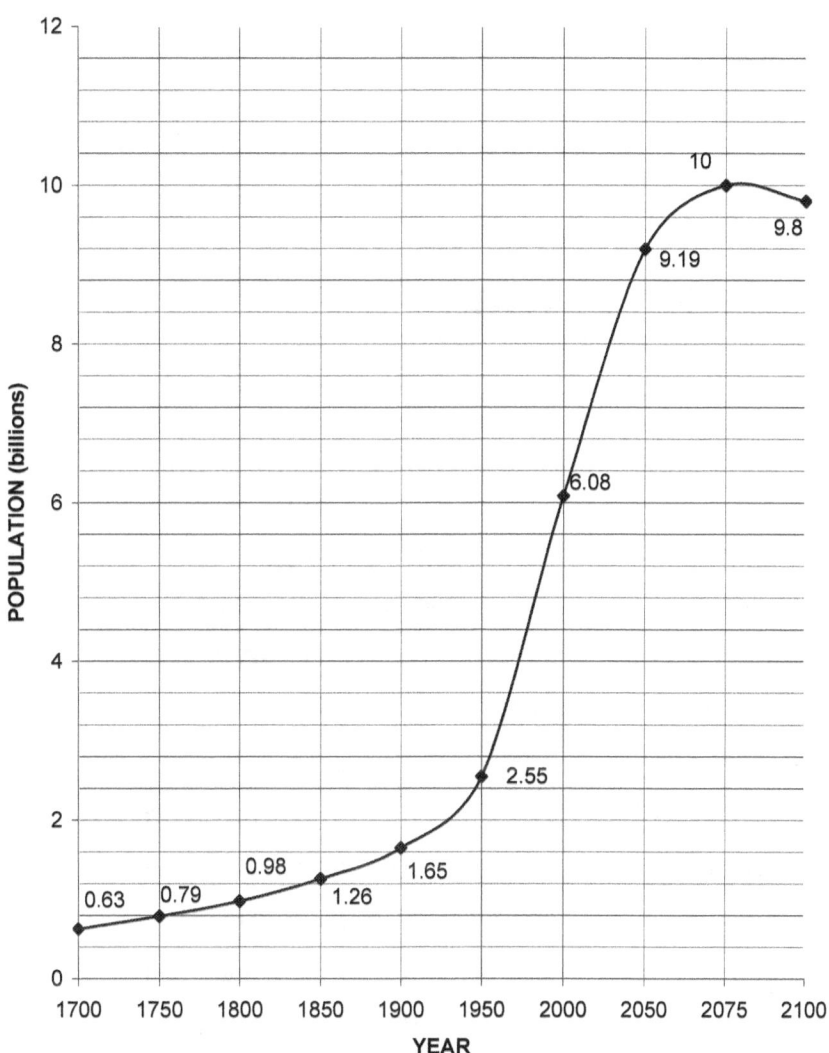

Note: Population growth from 2005 to 2100 is projected.

CURRENT STATUS

Today, the West holds a formidable lead over the East in cultural, economic, and political maturity, as well as stability. Its military capabilities are vastly superior to those of the East or any other region in the world. Western countries are wealthy and their economies, while subject to periodic fluctuations, are strong overall. The combined 2004 Gross Domestic Product (GDP)[1] of the five leading Western economies, those of the U.S., Germany, France, U.K., and Italy, was about $21 trillion. This was 1.3 times greater than that of the leading economies of the East, those of Japan, China, South Korea, India, and Indonesia. This is particularly significant because, in 2004, the combined total population of these five Asian countries was five times greater than that of the five Western countries. Thus, the average per capita GDP of the five Western countries was a robust $31,000 compared to a marginal $12,000 in the Eastern countries, reflecting the much greater prosperity of the

---

[1] The GDP is adjusted to reflect the relative values of local currencies. This adjustment is known as the purchasing Price Parity (PPP).

Westerners. The Western political influence is global, and nearly every country in the world is affected by the policies made in the West. The cultural and political outlook of the West is more compatible than that in the East. It is also better organized both militarily and politically. The North Atlantic Treaty Organization (NATO) binds the U.S., Canada, and Europe militarily by promoting mutual defense. Furthermore, the European Union (EU) unites most of Europe economically and politically, and also coordinates the countries' defenses. The Asian countries, on the other hand, are only loosely tied together through membership in organizations which, generally, promote and encourage economic, social, and cultural cooperation.

Yet in the East, when one only examines China's performance over the last decade, the magnitude of progress it has made is inescapably large. Its population grew by about 100 million, which is roughly one third the population of the U.S., and its GDP tripled to more than $7.25 trillion in 2004. A complete overhaul of the infrastructure was undertaken and a modest but growing nuclear deterrent, which is capable of reaching targets anywhere in the U.S., was developed. However, China is not alone in the East. Japan and South Korea are already highly developed industrial countries. Others, like India, Indonesia, Malaysia, and Thailand, are showing strong industrial development and economic growth. It is China, however, that appears to have the momentum, patience, and determination to become the nucleus of a powerful economic and political Eastern block which, in time, will be capable of challenging the West for global superiority.

The West, despite its apparently commanding position in the world, is vulnerable. On the surface, the partnership between the U.S. and Western Europe appears to be solid, but in reality, their long-term political objectives have been diverging for some time. The U.S. has a global perspective. It values its superior position in the world and is determined to maintain it. Its ultimate goal is to guarantee U.S. national security as well as preserve the West's superiority and way of life far into the future. The U.S. needs Europe to achieve this objective. Oppositely, Western Europe, particularly France and Germany, is focused on achieving a truly united Europe as represented by the EU that could some day rival the strength of the U.S. The EU has, at least in the foreseeable future, no global ambitions beyond those that protect Europe's interests. The United Kingdom, another key Western European nation, and Canada, both of whom enjoy a special, English-speaking relationship with the U.S., tend to sit on the fence. They tilt whichever way appears more in line with their own national interests.

Geographically, the East and the West are separated by Russia and the Islamic Belt countries. These nations form a key link. Hence, their policies and national interests will be a major factor in the East/West contention for superiority.

WEST

The West is comprised of all NATO and EU member nations. This includes the U.S., Canada, all West European nations (except Liechtenstein and Switzerland), some Eastern European countries, and Turkey, a total of 32 countries with a population of about 900 million in 2005. The languages and customs of the individual nations in this group may differ, however, except for Turkey, they all have a common Christian background.

UNITED STATES

The United States is the acknowledged leader of the West and, after the dissolution of the Soviet Union in 1991, the only superpower in the world.

Its population, which is estimated at roughly 300 million in 2005, is growing modestly at about 2.7 million per year. It is the third largest in the world, superceded only by China and India. Despite having a racially, ethnically, and religiously diverse population, the U.S. has not recently experienced any major social problems as a result. However, social problems may surface in the future, as the less privileged Hispanic and Asian segments of the population grow at a much faster rate than the rest of the population. Hispanics, as a result of higher fertility rates and continuing immigration, already make up about one-third of the populations in the states of California, Texas, and New Mexico. The U.S. demographic age profile has been relatively sound and stable since 1990. In 2005, 60 percent of the U.S. population was in the 20-64 work age group and 28 percent in the 0-19 youth age group. The 65+ senior age group was at 12 percent, which is low when compared to Western Europe. There are, however, some major changes on the horizon, as the U.S. population will start to age rapidly around 2010.

The U.S. economy is the largest in the world. Its GDP in 2004 was $11.75 trillion, and is growing at an average annual percentage rate of about 4 percent. The U.S.'s per capita GDP, in 2004, was the highest in the world at $40,100, which reflects the wealth of the average American. Individual wealth is a key factor in the U.S. economy, as consumer spending is responsible for about two-thirds of the Gross Domestic Product. Still, higher productivity and job outsourcing by U.S. companies has slowed the job growth. Higher trade and budget deficits, as well as accumulating national debt, are also sources of major concern. In the near future, an aging population will further strain the budget due to significantly increased expenditures on retirement and medical benefits. While these are legitimate concerns, the U.S. economy has shown considerable resilience as demonstrated in the aftermath of the 9-11 terrorist attack. Internationally, the U.S. has considerable control over the two largest lending institutions in the world, the International Monetary Fund (IMF) and the World Bank (WB), giving it significant economic and political leverage when dealing with other nations.

Concerning national defense, the U.S. is committed to maintaining the military superiority it has held since the end of the Cold War. U.S. strategic and conventional forces are superior, both quantitatively and qualitatively, to any nation in the world. The U.S. armed forces total 1.4 million active troops. The weapons available to them consist of about

8,000 tanks, 24,000 armored vehicles, 9,000 airplanes, 7,000 helicopters, and 200 warships, including nuclear powered aircraft carriers and submarines. The strategic forces comprise 550 Intercontinental Ballistic Missiles (ICBMs), 432 Submarine Launched Ballistic Missiles (SLBMs), and 92 bombers with a total of 11,519 nuclear warheads. The U.S. defense budget is seven times greater than that of the next nation (Russia) and greater than the combined defense budgets of the next twenty countries. The research and development (R&D) budget for new weapons alone is about equal to China's total defense budget. As part of this R&D process, the development of a missile defense system to protect the U.S. against a nuclear attack has been initiated. The U.S. armed forces have been modernized to provide a rapid and lethal response to any emergency. The communication, intelligence gathering, logistical, and training capabilities of the American armed forces are unparalleled. Additionally, military bases located in key areas around the world and vast transport capabilities provide the forces with global mobility.

However, despite the vast superiority in weapons, the U.S. would still find it difficult to fight two land wars simultaneously, as the armed forces have been reduced from 2 million troops during the Cold War to 1.4 million. In the war against Iraq, the U.S. needed to pressure friendly countries into contributing troops to a coalition force to ease the burden on its troops who are engaged in not only combat operations, but also in logistical support and peacekeeping. However, after lengthy negotiations, the troop contributions were still much smaller than requested. As the Iraqi conflict drags on, this weakness could be exploited by potential enemies, for example Iran and North Korea, to bolster defenses, increase weapon arsenals, or pursue policies contrary to U.S. interests, without risking retaliation on the ground. The U.S. is also in danger when fighting protracted, unconventional wars involving guerrilla warfare, insurgencies, and terrorism, as demonstrated in Vietnam and, most recently, in Iraq. Typically, the enemy has the advantage of receiving a large measure of support from the population and having more familiarity of the terrain. In this situation, the superior U.S. firepower is largely neutralized by the danger of inflicting massive civilian casualties.

On the international scene, the U.S. has an enormous impact on world affairs. The U.S. is the nominal head of NATO, a powerful and expanding military establishment, which includes most of Western Europe as well as many nations of Eastern Europe, including some bordering on Russia. Established under the North Atlantic Treaty (April 4, 1949), NATO was one of the most significant initiatives led by the U.S. during the Cold War against the threat of aggression by the Soviet Union. The Treaty provides for collective self-defense, considering an attack on any member an attack against all. The decision to use force is regulated by the member countries, and is based on unanimity and common accord. The decision to use force is then executed under U.S. command by an Integrated Military Force to which member countries contribute. Through its Western allies, the U.S. has close ties to the European Union and maintains major military bases in the U.K., Germany, Italy, Belgium, Spain, Portugal, and Iceland. The U.S. counts heavily on Western Europe to support its policy toward Russia and the Islamic states of the Greater Near East. It needs Europe to pull Russia closer to the Western sphere of influence; an issue the U.S. has difficulty with due to the lingering Russian distrust of U.S. intentions. On the Islamic front, the U.S. counts on Europe to back the American effort to transform the Greater Near East into a region where Western control predominates, free from Islamic extremism and hostility toward the State of Israel.

In Asia, the United States is closely tied to Japan through the 1953 U.S./ Japan Security Treaty, which allows it to maintain about 70,000 troops on Japanese soil. Under a Mutual Defense Treaty signed in 1953, the U.S. is also able to maintain a military presence in South Korea for an indefinite amount of time. The U.S. is able to point to Japan and South Korea as examples of the prosperity other countries in Asia can obtain through alliances with the West and, thus, try to counteract China's growing influence in this region of the world. In addition, the U.S. has a special relationship with the English-speaking nations of the U.K., Canada, and Australia, which transcends any alliances it may have with other countries.

The U.S. global policy is dictated by national security interests, the most fundamental of which is to create a secure, prosperous, and democratic world for the American people. As the only remaining superpower after the end of the Cold War, the U.S. has seen an opportunity to reconstruct the world's geo-political scene, and to establish a new, more favorable world order that the U.S. could control for decades to come. To accomplish this goal, a multifaceted approach has been employed using political, economic, and military initiatives. Politically, pressure is exerted on the authoritarian regimes to comply with accepted democratic principles and human rights standards. Threats of sanctions may be applied when international obligations are violated. If it is determined that a regime change is in order, support to internal or external opposition groups may be provided. The purpose of these actions is to isolate and weaken the regime. Economically, emphasis is placed on the need to adhere to a free market economy giving U.S. companies the opportunity to invest in their industries and thus gain a measure of economic leverage. At times resort to military threats or force may be required to achieve an important objective that cannot be readily achieved through political or economic means.

The window of opportunity to establish a kind of "Golden Age of the United States of America", characterized by unprecedented security and prosperity for all Americans, will not remain open forever. One might even argue that it is already partially shut, as Russia experiences a rapid revitalization and China marches forward at a faster pace than expected. North Korea has nuclear weapons and Iran may not be far behind in acquiring them. Decisions made in support of this central national goal do not always reflect the interests of other countries, including those of America's Western allies. These decisions, often made without prior consultations, lead to accusations of unilateralism by the United States' allies and the world community as a whole.

In President Bush's State of the Union address on 29 January 2002, the President laid out a near term road map for the U.S. This road map identified the initial key actions that need to be taken to secure a safer world for the United States. Iraq, Iran, and North Korea were singled out for pursuing weapons of mass destruction and deemed an "axis of evil". Without stating it directly, the priority U.S. policy became to pursue a regime change in these countries through any means necessary, including resort to force. The intention is to bring to power regimes that would be friendly to the U.S. and its interests, and to serve the purpose of supporting the ultimate U.S. objective of a more secure world.

American control of Iraq and Iran would assure that the supply of oil critical to U.S. industry would be available well into the middle of the century and would give the U.S. the potential to deny these resources to China, if deemed necessary. Furthermore, it would also open the gates to controlling Central Asia, which would further isolate Russia from the South and provide a pathway of allied countries leading to China's borders. Control of North Korea would eliminate its nuclear threat to the U.S. and its Asian allies, as well as put pressure on China directly from the Asian mainland.

Iraq was considered the preferred starting point. Saddam Hussein's Iraq regime was not popular in the region. It waged a long and brutal war with its neighbor Iran in the 1980's, and then invaded Kuwait in 1990. Saddam Hussein's regime also brutally suppressed its Shiite and Kurd populations. These factors, combined with Iraq's possession of the third largest oil reserves in the world, made Iraq a valuable prize.

Furthermore, successful, democratic Iraq would serve a positive example to the rest of the states in the region, contribute to a more peaceful Middle East, and diminish the Arab threat to Israel. On the pretext that Iraq was harboring weapons of mass destruction, Operation Iraq Freedom was launched on March 20, 2003 by a combined U.S. and British force. This operation lacked UN support and approval. Some allies, particularly France and Germany, disapproved of the action and refused to participate in the operation. Saddam Hussein's regime collapsed in several weeks and the war was officially declared over on May 1, 2003. Saddam Hussein was captured on December 13th of the same year, however, no evidence of weapons of mass destruction was ever found.

Despite the overthrow of Hussein and the installation of an Iraqi interim government, an unexpectedly strong insurgency has ensued. The insurgency is led by Saddam loyalists and Islamic militants, some with ties to al-Quaeda, and continues to inflict casualties on U.S. forces, Iraqi police, National Guard troops, and civilians. Reconstruction is moving at a painfully slow pace as violence and chaos persist. The insurgency has moored about 150,000 U.S. troops in Iraq and the surrounding region, and is costing the U. S. about $4 billion per month.

As the current situation in Iraq develops, any action against Iran and North Korea, the other members of the "axis of evil", would most likely have to be limited to diplomatic pressure, sanctions, or, in a case of high threat to U.S. national security, to aerial bombardment.

In the course of pressing its primary long-range objective of a friendlier, more manageable world order, the U.S. also seeks to address the immediate threats of terrorism, proliferation of WMD, and potential disruption of oil supplies.

Terrorists can be affiliated with any nation, ethnic group, or religion. However, the foremost terrorist threat to the U.S. and the West comes from individuals or groups with roots in the Islamic Belt countries. The 9-11 attack on the U.S. was planned and executed by nationals of some of these countries under the control of the al-Quaeda terrorist organization. Despite previous acts of terrorism committed against the U.S. by Islamic extremists, the magnitude of the 9-11 attack shocked the U.S. and prompted the assault on Afghanistan in 2002 to eliminate the training bases of the al-Quaeda terrorist organization under the leadership of Osama bin Laden. The Homeland Security Strategy for combating terrorism at home and abroad was developed in 2003. The cost of terrorism defense is high. $38 billion was budgeted in FY 2003 for homeland security, and state and local governments across the country expect to spend an additional $2 billion on security per year. Including FY2006, the total spent in Iraq and Afghanistan for fighting and reconstruction, as well as on other world-wide efforts against terrorism, will exceed $300 billion.

As the war on terrorism continues, its cost is significantly contributing to a growing national budget deficit. Nevertheless, despite these efforts to combat terrorism, terrorist acts against the U. S. and its interests undoubtedly will continue, as the root causes of terrorism remain unaddressed. In essence, rapidly growing populations in Islamic Belt countries, coupled with unemployment and governments that mostly cater to the powerful elite, create a volatile environment in which extremist Islamic groups can readily find recruits. Anger among the disproportionately young populations (most as high as 30-35 percent in the 15-29 age group) is roused by Islamic rhetoric, prevalent in media, mosques, and schools, that blames the West, as the former colonial masters and supporters of their corrupt and often oppressive governments, for the poor state of affairs. The U.S., as the leader of the West and supporter of the Moslem despised State of Israel, is singled out particularly. Some terrorist organizations are known, while countless others operate underground, only to identify themselves in order to take credit for a terrorist act. Most terrorists see themselves as holy warriors, fighting an evil West that infringes on their sovereignty, exploits their resources, tramples on their culture, and ridicules their religion. They find sympathy for their cause not only among the disenfranchised masses, but also in high government circles and among wealthy citizens who provide financial support. The U.S., and other Western countries, are taking the basic steps to combat terrorism, which include a greater awareness of the threat, heightening security of high value targets, increasing intelligence, and greater scrutiny of financial transactions involving terrorist linked organizations. However, terrorism will remain a problem for the U.S. and the rest of the West for some time as the terrorists have found a weakness in the West's armor and it is highly unlikely that they will relinquish it without substantial progress in addressing their major grievances of injustice toward Moslems and West's interference in their part of the world. The U.S., with its close ties to Israel and its need to stay in the region to protect the oil supplies, is in no position to accommodate them. Thus, terrorism is unlikely to abate soon.

The U.S. supremacy in conventional warfare has prompted adversaries to seek unconventional, asymmetric means as a deterrent against a U.S. attack. Rogue states and terrorist groups, equipped with biological, chemical, and/or nuclear weapons of mass destruction (WMD), pose a significant threat to the U.S. and its Western allies. Thus, stopping the proliferation of WMD through global black market networks and the sale of "dual use" equipment, with both industrial and nuclear weapons applications, is a top priority for the United States. Additionally, the U.S. is trying to end the confidential collaboration on WMD between states, such as the exchange of North Korea's ballistic missile technology for Pakistan's nuclear technology.

North Korea is a prime candidate to be involved in proliferation of WMD, having already developed a small number of atomic weapons and possessing the capability to produce more. North Korea's indigenously developed two-stage Taepo Dong 2 missile, equipped with a nuclear warhead, is capable of striking Alaska and Hawaii. A three-stage long range missile, currently under development, could reach most parts of the continental United States. In addition, North Korea is suspected of having built a uranium enrichment facility in a secret location that is capable of producing 2 to 3 atomic bombs per year, some of which could be supplied to other rogue states or terrorist groups. U.S. diplomatic pressure on North Korea to dismantle its nuclear program has not been effective. A preemptive aerial strike to destroy the nuclear facilities would risk either a nuclear retaliation or a protracted, and costly, land war with a one million-strong North Korean army. With U.S. involvement continuing in Iraq and Afghanistan, the nation would be hard pressed to reinforce in any significant way the 34,000 troops in South Korea and the 70,000 troops stationed in Japan. Outside of the U.K., West European support would be unlikely, and South Korea may be a reluctant participant against the North. Japan, restricted by its Constitution to a self-defensive capability, may, at best, provide some logistics support. The North Korean nuclear standoff illustrates the weakening position of the U.S. in Asia. At the same time it highlights the strength of China with armed forces numbering two and one half million troops, backed by an advanced nuclear capability.

Iran has also benefited from Pakistan's proliferation of nuclear technology. Iran's capability to produce weapons grade enriched uranium puts it a step away from developing a nuclear weapon. The Iranian developed Shahab-3, a medium range ballistic missile with a range of about 930 miles equipped with a nuclear warhead, would put U.S. forces in the Persian Gulf, the Arabian Peninsula, Iraq, and Afghanistan under a nuclear threat. Israel is also well within the range of this missile. The nuclear capability would give Iran, a government strongly opposed to the U.S. and its policies, the leading power position in the Greater Near East. Iran insists that its nuclear program is designed to generate power for civilian use and the government has allowed the UN to inspect its facilities. The ability of the U.S. to prevent Iran from becoming a nuclear state is limited. Iran, with a population of roughly 70 million, half a million of which is in the armed forces, would be a difficult opponent. In the event of a U.S. preemptive strike against its nuclear facilities, Iran could use its large inventory of Scud type missiles to close the Straits of Hormuz to oil traffic. Disruption of oil supplies from the Persian Gulf, if continued for an extended period, would have a devastating effect on the world's economies, particularly that of the U.S. which depends on the Persian Gulf imports for 25 percent of its oil consumption. The U.S. dependency on imported oil is a glaring weakness that is exploited by states and terrorist groups alike. The need for uninterrupted oil supplies often forces the U.S. to politically and militarily support key oil exporting states in the Islamic Belt with poor records on democracy and human rights that are counter to the stated foreign policy goals of the U.S. Department of State. In the coming decades, the dependency on Islamic oil will only increase as oil production in other parts of the world, with the exception of Russia, decreases.

Since 9-11, the United States has taken on a more aggressive stance toward the world. Questions remain, however, about how long the U.S. can sustain the actions taken and those contemplated, considering the high costs of the military campaigns and the casualties sustained by U.S. soldiers.

WESTERN-ORIENTED EUROPE (EU)

Western-oriented Europe, which is led by Germany, France, and the U.K., includes some of the wealthiest and strongest nations in the world. Germany has the fifth largest economy in the world, while France and the U.K. are both nuclear powers. Together, with fourteen other Western European and eight Eastern European countries, they are the European Union. The EU was first established in 1952. Initially it consisted of six countries (Belgium, France, Federal Republic of Germany, Italy, Luxembourg, and Netherlands), it was known as the European Community. In the next 52 years, it grew to a total of 25 countries, from both Western and Eastern Europe. Committed to working together for peace and prosperity, the EU coordinates the member countries' policies in economics, internal affairs, foreign relations, security, and defense. The EU is unique in that its member states have created shared institutions, to which they delegate some of their sovereignty, in order to allow that decisions of joint-European interest can be made democratically at the European regional level. The EU has built a single European market, launched a single European currency (the Euro), and strengthened Europe's voice in the world. As such, the EU is moving in the direction of representing Europe as one state. The EU, one of the world's largest trading partners with a total Gross Domestic Product of about $11.65 trillion in 2004 (almost equal to that of the U.S.), is a major player on the world scene. Although it has a global outlook, its main concern is the security of Europe and the state of affairs in the regions bordering it, specifically the Middle East, Russia, and North Africa.

During the Cold War, Western Europe followed U.S. foreign policy and firmly supported NATO. With the breakup of the Soviet Union, the Soviet threat to Europe vanished and, consequently, NATO's political and military role has diminished. In addition, the responsibilities of NATO and the EU have, to some extent, started to overlap. European nations, reflecting their population's desire for peace and stability, are increasingly looking to the EU to set foreign policy and defense goals. This, in turn, has made it difficult for the U.S. to deal with the EU member states one-on-one. As Western European nations, particularly France, Germany, Belgium, and Spain, pursue a more independent course, some of their foreign policy decisions are not fully in line with U.S. national interests. By deciding not to support the U.S. policy in Iraq, France and Germany in a way wanted to break the cycle of blindly following U.S. initiatives and, thus, show the independence of the EU. The U.K., which has a special relationship with the U.S., tends to support U.S. policies more often than the others. In the Iraq conflict, the U.K. backed the U.S. policy to remove Saddam Hussein from power and provided troops for Operation Iraqi Freedom. While they differ on some issues, the U.K. and the U.S. have been able to arrive at a consensus on matters of great importance to them through more unilateral consultations. The Eastern European countries, which joined the EU after the dissolution of the Soviet Union, are primarily concerned with improving their nations' economies and raising the standard of living for their citizens. Generally, they play a lesser role in international affairs. However, some, particularly Poland, supported the U.S. policy on Iraq and have provided sizable troop contingents to maintain security in the country. On the whole, Europe, as represented by the EU, has become more independent from the U.S. and it does not share the ultimate goal of the United States to bring permanent security to the West through judicious control of the world.

As the threat to Europe diminished, economic and social issues are beginning to take center stage for both individual European nations and the EU. Much of Europe's new outlook can be attributed to the demographic changes that are taking place in the region. In general, Europe's population has stabilized around 730 million. The 0-19 age group is decreasing as fertility rates drop. The 20-64 working age group is peaking and will begin to decline after 2010. On the other hand, the 65+ senior age group is increasing sharply and is approaching 20 percent of the population in most European countries. Europe's older generation experienced the horrors of World War II as children, and, hence, they place high value on peace. They see conflicts and wars as the personal ambitions of leaders who cause the general population great suffering in pursuit of their goals. As parents and grandparents, this generation exerts a significant influence on Europe's younger generations. Evidence of this can be seen in the peace marches held by thousands of Europeans of all ages in many cities across Europe prior to the start of Iraqi hostilities. Also, much to the dismay of the United States, European governments raid their defense budgets to provide benefits to the elderly, instead of using the funds to modernize their military capabilities, which would be of greater use to NATO. However, despite the lack of a full commitment to adapt their armed forces to modern needs, France, U.K., Germany, and Italy have some of the strongest military capabilities in the world.

Currently, Western European economies are sound and growing at a modest rate of 1 to 3 percent per year. Inflation rates are also low; only 2 to 3 percent annually. Unemployment, generally in the 8 to 10 percent range, is an ongoing problem. The economic growth rates in Eastern European countries are somewhat higher (3 to 6 percent), as they try to strengthen their industries in the post-Cold War era. Their inflation and unemployment rates are also higher than those in Western Europe. However, both Eastern and Western Europe's demographic projections show their populations declining and aging dramatically in 15 to 20 years, which could trigger a long period of economic downturn. Due to the increasing interdependence of economies, the economic slowdown in Europe could possibly spill over to other countries, especially the U.S.

The growing economies of Western Europe make it an attractive destination for Moslem immigrants; consequently, the sizeable Moslem populations in these countries are continuing to grow. High fertility rates among Moslem women have resulted in the rapid growth of Moslem citizens, particularly in countries like France (8 percent), Germany (4 percent), Netherlands (4.5 percent), and Spain (2 percent). Thus, their policies toward Moslem countries are influenced somewhat by these circumstances. Hostility towards Moslem movements may lead to retaliation by terrorist groups similar to the March 11, 2004 bombing in Madrid that killed 191 people. More terrorist attacks could, conceivably, result in a nationalistic backlash in these countries as tensions between different ethnic and religious groups rise.

Most EU countries, with the exception of the U.K. and Norway, have very limited energy resources, beyond coal and nuclear power, and, therefore, they must import their oil and gas from the Middle East, Russia, and North Africa. As the world's leading exporter of gas and second leading exporter of oil, Russia is increasingly becoming Europe's critical and most dependable supplier of energy. This has led to much friendlier diplomatic relations between France, Germany, and Russia. Russia, in turn, has been relatively receptive to the growth of the EU and considers it a welcome counterbalance to U.S. power.

CANADA

Canada is another country that is firmly in the Western sphere. Majority English-speaking, it has always had a special relationship with the U.S. Nonetheless, like Western Europe, Canada has recently acted independently of the U.S. in world affairs on a number of important issues. Canada/U.S. relations were strained in 2003 when Canada did not support the invasion of Iraq and refused to join the U.S. led coalition force. In 2005, their relationship suffered a further setback when Canada chose not to participate in the U.S. anti-ballistic missile shield program.

With a population of about 32 million and a GDP of $1 trillion in 2004, Canada is a highly developed industrial country and an important U.S. trading partner. The countries are further linked by the North American Free Trade Agreement (NAFTA). Rich in oil and gas, it provides the U.S. with 15 percent of its energy consumption.

Canada's major domestic issue has been to keep the country united in spite of the friction between the English and French speaking segments of the population. At times this leads to a separatist movement by the predominantly French province of Quebec.

TURKEY

In order to bolster the southern flank of Europe against the threat of the former Soviet Union, Turkey was admitted as a full member of NATO in 1952. Since then, with the help of the U.S., it has significantly developed its military strength, and is now numerically the largest conventional military force in European NATO. Turkey, however, has periodically experienced internal political instability, and it has shown a tendency to act solely in its own interest in world affairs, regardless of international pressure to change course. Frequently, the Turkish military has interfered in domestic politics and it continues to have a powerful voice today.

As part of NATO, Moslem Turkey did contribute troops for peacekeeping efforts in Afghanistan. However, Turkey refused to permit the U.S. to use its bases as a launching pad for the war against Iraq.

Recently, Turkey sought to enter negotiations to become a member of the European Union. So far, the discussions have not led to any concrete steps toward membership due to the concerns of some EU members that Turkey does not fully adhere to democratic principles. There is also concern surrounding the impact that the Turkish Moslem population of 70 million would have on the EU.

U.S. plans to give Turkey a greater political role in the Greater Near East have not yet materialized, as regional governments continue to harbor a fear of Turkish intentions.

EAST

The East consists of all the countries in Eastern Asia besides Russia. With the exception of Japan, the countries of the East are still in the developing stage, both economically and politically. However, nearly the entire region is experiencing a rapid and dynamic change, and is on the threshold of becoming a worthy challenger to the West. China, in particular, has made exceptional progress in the last two decades and it appears to have the momentum it needs to break out of the pack, and to become a world power.

CHINA

Since the end of World War II, China has been a powerful, yet sometimes unpredictable, force in East Asia. A period of harsh Communist rule followed Mao Zedong's victory in 1949 over the Nationalist forces led by General Chiang Kai-shek. During this span, China was able to maintain a position of strength and importance in East Asia, despite internal struggles, strained, adverse relations with Taiwan, and a general lack of national direction by Mao Zedong and those who followed him. It was not until the 1980's, however, when, under the leadership of Deng Xiaoping, China's drive to achieve its full potential went into high gear, with a substantial reinterpretation of the Communist ideology and comprehensive economic changes. Through a set of sweeping reforms, China skillfully moved toward a market economy while at the same time politically retaining authoritarian rule. Recently, China has shown that it can use to its advantage the newly acquired economic and political power.

In some ways, it has already overshadowed Japan as the most influential country in Asia. Eventually, it will be strong enough to challenge the West on the world scene.

With a population of 1.3 billion in 2005, China is the most populous country in the world. It will continue to hold this position until about 2035, when China will be overtaken by India. Slightly larger in geographic area than the United States, China's population is about 4.5 times that of the U.S. China's 2005 population age profile has the signature of a moderately developed country, with a decreasing 0-19 youth age group at 30 percent and a rising 65+ senior age group at 8 percent. The 20-64 working age group is at 62 percent and is projected to peak at 64 percent around 2015. This age distribution indicates a substantially more stable future for China as the most volatile young segment of the population decreases. At the time of the Beijing Tiananmen Square student riots of 1989, the youth age group was about 40 percent of the population, which is about 25 percent greater than it is today. Stability is an important factor in China's continued development as an economic and military power in Asia. Additionally, this stability will be critical to China's future role in the international community.

China's economic growth during the past two decades has propelled it to the forefront of the world's economic scene. China's $7.3 trillion economy in 2004 was second only to the U.S. at $11.75 trillion as measured by the GDP. China's offer of economic incentives for businesses, which include lower taxes, has led to rapidly expanding foreign investments which now account for a large share of China's exports. Much of the initial investment came from Chinese living in Hong Kong, Singapore, Taiwan and Indonesia. As China showed increasing internal political stability, additional investments from Japan, the U.S., and Europe followed. The size of China's labor market is enormous and the country's low per capita GDP of about $5,600 in 2004 (compared to U.S. 2004 per capita GDP of $40,100) indicates that labor is relatively cheap. Cheaper labor and quality workmanship make their well-made, but lower priced goods, attractive in the world market and, also, help importing countries keep their inflation in check. Reminiscent of the Industrial Revolution during the 1700's in Europe, the demand for Chinese goods has become the driving force of its economic expansion, as a mostly agricultural country is transformed into an industrial giant. Many peasants have left their land and have moved to industrial urban areas seeking jobs. Similar problems to those encountered in Europe during the Industrial Revolution accompany the migration of workers. These issues include poor working conditions, pollution, and crime. However, development has not been equal in all parts of the country, and a large income gap exists between rural and urban workers. Rural areas have high unemployment rates and lack transport and other infrastructure. Much of China's output today is for export which results in substantial trade surpluses with other countries, particularly the U.S., which is a heavy importer of Chinese goods. As China becomes wealthier and develops a middle class, domestic consumption will increase and play a greater role in the economy. Higher living standards across a broad spectrum of the population and reduced unemployment will undoubtedly contribute to economic and political stability. In 2001, China was admitted to the World Trade Organization (WTO), which recognized China's importance in the world economy. As economic strength has become a major indicator of power, it can be concluded that China's ascent to a position as a major global power is inevitable.

As the Chinese economy grows, so does its demand for oil. Currently, about one third of China's oil consumption is imported, mostly from the Middle East, as its own sizable oil reserves have remained largely untapped. Since world consumption levels are approaching current feasible production levels, the unexpectedly high demand for oil from China is largely responsible for the steady increase in oil prices. To reduce its dependence on Middle East oil, Chinese energy companies are turning to Russia, Canada, and Venezuela as potential suppliers to assure its industrial complex has the energy it needs.

China is also one of the world's growing military powers. However, despite China's increase in defense spending to roughly $60 billion[2] in 2005 and the modernization of its armed forces, it is proceeding at a measured pace so as not to interfere with economic growth or risk a premature confrontation with the U.S. With a world high 2.5 million troops under arms and nuclear-armed missiles, China's military strength is superior to that of any other country in East Asia. Nonetheless, currently it is substantially inferior to that of the United States. China has been relaying on Russia for heavy armaments, including tanks, aircraft, ships and submarines. Some of the armaments provided by Russia are technologically inferior and would be less reliable in a combat situation. In order to maintain a viable deterrent, China has a modest strategic force that consists of 20 CSS-4 intercontinental land based missiles with nuclear

---

[2] The officially announced figure is about $30 billion, but actual defense spending more likely is double that amount.

warheads (also called DF-5 ICBMs) that can reach targets anywhere in the U.S. It also has another 230 nuclear weapons deployed (or that can be deployed) on aircraft, missiles, or submarines; however, these weapons have only regional capabilities. Among them is the CSS-5 medium range missile with multi-head capability to counter the joint U.S./Japan defense capability. Its CSS-6/CSS-7 short-range missiles are mostly deployed opposite Taiwan. China's nuclear armed forces are currently limited to one XIA type 092 nuclear powered and nuclear ballistic missile equipped submarine (SSBN) that can carry 12 SLBMs with a range of 1055 miles.

However, the submarine has reactor and acoustic problems, which keeps it in regional waters.

Currently, China's military forces are strong enough to protect it against its neighboring countries and to enforce its one-China policy with regard to Taiwan. The nuclear deterrent keeps the U.S. in check. China is well aware that it needs to develop its own modern and technologically advanced defense industry before it will be able to compete with the U.S. When China's economy is strong enough, it will be ready to direct a greater portion of its GDP from civilian consumption and capital reinvestment to military expansion.

China's foreign policy is very much influenced by its long-term goal of becoming the undisputed power in the East. Its approach is to exercise patience and to proceed one step at a time. Its current priorities are to develop a strong economy, become a wealthy country, and instill a sense of national unity and purpose among its population. Only after these goals are achieved will China proceed with development of a strong military industrial base that is capable of producing advanced military systems for its armed forces. In the meantime, it exercises self-restraint, participates constructively in international affairs (including the UN), avoids alliances, and maintains good relations with neighboring countries. It adheres to a policy of non-interference and urges others to do the same. As far as Taiwan is concerned, China continues to espouse the one-China policy, but it avoids setting a timetable for it to revert to China.

In an attempt to polish its image on the international scene, as well as help to instill a sense of national pride, China has rigorously pursued a policy of hosting a series of international events; for example, the 2008 Summer Olympics in Beijing and the 2010 World Exposition in Shanghai. These events will facilitate China's integration into the international community. China hopes that visitors to these events will go back to their countries and marvel at the showpiece of the world China has become, akin to the traders who returned to Western Europe from China during the early periods of its greatness.

Thus, the giant-to-be waits with patience and confidence that, eventually its return to greatness will materialize.

JAPAN

Japan's post-World War II economic recovery was, by any standards, remarkable. Less than five years after signing the U.S./Japan Peace and Security Treaties, Japan's drive towards national prosperity moved forward and produced remarkable results in a short time. New technologies and manufacturing methods were rapidly undertaken with great success. A shrewd trade policy, which caused some tensions with U.S., gave Japan a larger share in Western markets. The economic growth continued through the 1970's and 1980's, despite accusations of protectionism fueled by close involvement of the Japanese government in the country's banking and industry. This remarkable period of economic expansion, with annual growth averaging over 4 percent, made Japan the world's second largest economy after U.S. by 1990. During the 1990's, Japan suffered an economic downturn that was marked by scandals involving government officials, banks, and leaders of industry. Banks closed under the weight of bad loans, unemployment rose, real estate values dropped, and many businesses failed. The 1998 Asian economic crisis caused the worst recession in Japan since World War II. Japan's economic growth stalled, and the implementation of structural reforms has been disappointingly slow.

Japan's demographic profile does not favor an economic resurgence, as the population is rapidly aging and the working age segment of the population is declining sharply. Overall, Japan's population growth has slowed. It will peak at about 128 million in 2007 and decline to about 100 million by the year 2050. During the same period, the 65+ age group will increase from about 20 percent to 34 percent, one of the highest percentages worldwide. Between 2005 and 2020, the rate of increase in this population segment will be the steepest in the world. On the other hand, its working population age group (20-64 years old) will decrease from 60 percent to 55 percent during the same period. Because of these demographic changes Japan faces a heavy elderly support burden at a time when the family support system, so prevalent before World War II, has slowly been eroding as attitudes change. The social burden of supporting an aging population will have a major impact on Japan and its economy as fewer working people have to support an increasing elderly population, which will leave less money for them to spend on consumer goods. Thus, Japan faces challenges in the health care system, elderly care, pensions, and other social support systems.

In addition, Japan, as a heavily industrialized nation, is also particularly vulnerable in the energy sector. Practically all oil is imported. In 2005, 88 percent will come from the volatile Middle East. Any sustained disruptions in Middle Eastern oil supplies would, consequently, have a seriously negative effect on Japan's economy. Rising oil prices will adversely affect the Japanese economy, even without oil supply disruptions.

Despite the unfavorable economic and demographic trends, Japan is currently, still not in a "crisis situation". It remains wealthy, with a per capita GDP among the highest in the world ($29,400 in 2004), and Japan's 127 million people enjoy one of the highest standards of living in the industrialized world. Japan's GDP of $3.7 billion in 2004 ranks third in the world. Even with low growth or zero growth in GDP, Japan's per capita income will continue to rise because its population will shortly start to decline.

Japan's goal is to remain a strong economic and political power in Asia. However, it is well aware of the rapidly growing giant across the Yellow Sea. Unlike China, which is fully independent of any world powers, Japan depends heavily on the U.S. for protection and foreign policy coordination. It is this independence that allows China to claim a superior status among countries both inside and outside of Asia.

Overall, Japan has lost considerable influence in Asia and around the world over the past decade. Japan's problems include that its economic superpower status is in question, its defense system relies too heavily on the U.S., it has been intimidated by North Korea's missile capabilities, and China, Asia's rising star, cannot be counted as one of its friends. Only in the economic arena has cooperation between China and Japan been good.

Japan's military capabilities are considerable, but designed to be defensive in nature. Its armed forces are modern, and its defense expenditures are about 1 percent of GDP, roughly the same as France and Germany. Japan has about 240,000 troops in its Self Defense Forces (SDF). The core military hardware consists of about 1,000 tanks, 400 fighter aircraft, and 75 warships, which include 16 submarines.

Unlike China, Japan does not have a clear future goal. It could adhere to status quo, with the goal to remain a strong economic power, but continue to rely on U.S. for military protection and foreign policy guidance. It could also, as some Japanese conservatives prefer, re-arm militarily and strike its own foreign policy, with the ultimate goal of being a stronger, more independent force in Asia. The latter option would likely be met with opposition from the U.S., China, and other countries in East Asia who Japan treated badly in the past, especially, in the period before and during World War II. However, if the threat of North Korean missiles is not resolved to Japan's satisfaction, it may have little choice but to acquire its own offensive capability. Nonetheless, the U.S. would prefer that Japan remain a close ally and take a more active role in international affairs, particularly in Asia. It would like Japan, along with South Korea, Australia, and other friendly countries in the Pacific, to act as a counterbalance to China, and, also, to protect U.S. interests in the region.

INDIA

India, which has a geographic area only one-third the size of China's, has one of the highest birth rates in Asia and is projected to surpass China in total population by approximately 2035 which would make it the most populous state in the world. In the next 30 years, India will add 400 million people to its population. As with most other developing nations, India's population is youthful, with about 40 percent of its people 19 years or younger in 2005. Very high percentages in the 0-19 age group tend to produce a general state of instability in those countries. Oppositely, its 65+ age group in 2005 is a very modest 5 percent of the population. The working age group is still on the rise, and will reach 55 percent by 2005.

Since gaining its independence from Britain in 1947, India has been on a bumpy road and has not been able to match China in its economic development. Some of India's shortcomings can be attributed to sharp social and religious differences among its population, as well as several wars with its neighbor, Pakistan, over control of the disputed territory of Kashmir.

Only about 60 percent of Indians are literate, as compared to about 85 percent in China. This, to a great extent, is due to the caste system practiced by Hindus. Hindus make up India's largest religious group, roughly 85 percent of the population. According to Hinduism, a person belongs to the caste of his parents and is not expected to leave it. Consequently,

Hindus often do the same kind of work that their parents did. Social contacts with members of other castes are also limited. Although many educated Hindus of various castes now mix together freely as a result of education and industrialization, the remnants of the caste system have had a dampening effect on full industrial development and economic progress for all of India. India's wealth is controlled by a small elite minority. Most Indians are poor by Western standards, as the 2004 per capita GDP of only about $3,100 indicates. However, India's 2004 GDP was at $3.3 trillion, which makes it the fourth largest economy in the world. The GDP continues to grow at a healthy annual rate of about 6 percent. Roughly half of the economy revolves around agriculture, although recently strides have been made to increase the industrial and service sectors particularly in computer technology and programming. India's standard of living has been improving steadily, but more slowly than some of its neighbors. However, in the long run, India has the natural resources and people to potentially become a significant force in Asia. The key to India's success is for the Indian government to involve all racial and religious segments of the population in the development of the country. In the next 50 years, India's population demographics will change substantially as the 0-19 age group, currently at a very high 40 percent, will decrease to about 25 percent of the total population. This will strike a better balance for economic development and political stability in the country. Another important factor will also be the progress made toward settlement of the differences over Kashmir with Pakistan.

Militarily, at 1.3 million troops, India has the third largest active armed forces in the world. India also possesses a modest nuclear capability. The current defense budget of about $15 billion for 2005 is small compared to Japan's and China's, but more than likely it will increase substantially with further economic development and industrialization of the country in the future.

India's relationship toward the U.S. is characterized by caution, partly due to U.S. support of Pakistan and partly due to its apprehension of dealing with a Western power, as memories of its colonial past have not been fully erased by time. The country avoids the expansion of Western influence; instead it prefers an independent foreign policy that gives it more freedom in developing its political relationship toward the other countries in Asia and around the world. Consequently, India prefers to depend on its own industry or Russia, which is less likely to attach political strings, for military hardware. Eventually, India has the potential to challenge China for the leadership of Asia, provided it can solve its long standing social problems, some with religious overtones, and instill a sense of national unity in its population. However, history shows that religious problems are difficult to solve, as they often involve changing the religion itself, which can prove to be quite difficult.

INDONESIA

Indonesia, the world's most populous Moslem nation, is another rapidly developing country in Asia. Its GDP in 2004 was $825 billion, and is growing at an average annual percentage rate of about 5 percent. Indonesia is rich in natural resources including oil, natural gas, tin, copper, coal, gold, silver, and timber. As the fourth most populous country in the world, it has a history of political instability. To some degree, this is due to democratic institutions that are still maturing, a strong military influence over the government, separatist movements, and rising Moslem extremism. Since gaining its independence from the Dutch in 1949, Indonesia has made great strides to establish itself as the foremost voice of the Islamic world in East Asia.

OTHER EASTERN COUNTRIES

Besides China, India, Japan, and Indonesia, the remaining countries of East Asia, which include South Korea, Philippines, Malaysia, Thailand, Myanmar, and Vietnam, are developing nations that substantially contribute to the growth of East Asia. Recently, the GDP of these countries grew on the average about 5 percent per year. None of these countries, however, have the short term potential to become leaders in this important and rapidly developing part of the world.

EAST/WEST LINKS

The geographic separation between the East and the West, which is highlighted by the lack of common borders between their countries, has produced cultural differences between them that are difficult to overcome even today despite the technological advances in land, air, and sea transportation systems. In earlier periods, invasions played a role in cultural exchanges; later, colonialism and world wars contributed. Most of these cultural exchanges, however, have involved the subjugation of one country or group of people by another. This considerably reduced the prospects of full and lasting cultural transformations. It is these differences among cultures that often lead to disagreements between the East and the West.

Geographically, only Russia and the Islamic Belt countries provide a land link between East and West. As such, they will have a major influence on the result of the anticipated conflict between these two geographically and culturally removed regions.

A neutral Russia and an Islamic world hostile to the West will be in East's favor; just as a subdued Islamic world and a Western-oriented Russia would favor the West.

RUSSIA

Russia is unique in some ways, as it does not belong to either the East or the West. Although culturally closer to the West, its Slavic population sets it apart from the West.

Despite the collapse of the Soviet Union in 1991, which resulted in the loss of one-third of its territory as 14 Russian Republics declared independence, Russia remains a major world power. In a relatively short period, Russia underwent a dramatic transition from a totalitarian Communist regime during the Cold War confrontation with the West to a government-managed democracy with strong nationalistic overtones.

Russia has concentrated on domestic reforms and improving its economy since the end of its superpower status. In the international arena, Russia is focused on working more closely with the West, regaining its international influence, and improving relations with its former Republics. Above all, cautious behavior is exercised in order not to amplify its weakened position in the world.

On the whole, the Russian people have responded favorably to this approach, and Russia's President Putin is a popular leader, who enjoys the people's support and even admiration. After the period of regret and disillusionment at the loss of world prestige, which followed the collapse of the Soviet Union, a nationalistic sentiment prevails currently among the majority of Russian people. They support the government's firm-handed methods of consolidating the country and bringing its control under a strong presidential leadership, despite the fact that this action may disturb some in the West. It is not particularly important to the Russian people whether or not full democratic principles are being employed, or exactly which methods are used. For that matter, they are not strong proponents of Western style democracy or liberal capitalism, and they remain suspicious of the West, particularly the U.S. After a long period of uncertainty, the Russians trust their government, and most feel that the freedoms they now enjoy and the progress made in developing a free market economy are not in jeopardy. Russia's leaders and politicians are now democratically elected, even if doubts remain about the full legitimacy and fairness of the elections. Some progress has been made by the current administration in overhauling Russia's entrenched monopolies and attracting much needed foreign investment. For example, in 2004, Russia essentially took control over the oil giant Yukos, whose president was arrested a year earlier on charges of fraud and tax evasion. Most importantly, however, is that the country's identity is beginning to evolve in the direction that the majority of Russian people are willing to support.

To regain its high status in the world, the Russian government must undertake painful reforms, with the full participation of the Russian people, as it overhauls the industrial and financial base as well as attempts to incorporate new technologies and eliminate waste. This is necessary in order to be able to compete economically with other countries, particularly those of the West. In addition to attracting foreign investment, Russians must invest in their own country, too. Currently, Russia shows healthy economic growth largely due to increased demand for its natural resources, primarily its oil and gas. Based on recent reports, Russia's oil reserves are estimated to be 120 billion barrels (almost double previous estimates), which makes Russia second to Saudi Arabia. Most Russian oil firms have enough oil reserves to maintain current output for at least 40 years, while few Western firms have enough to cover 10 years production. The production and exportation of oil and gas has increased significantly in Russia during the last 5 years, and has contributed heavily to Russia's average economic growth rate of 5 percent during this period. Along with Saudi Arabia, Iraq, Iran, Kuwait, and United Arab Emirates, Russia is one of the last remaining oil players in the world. However, in order for sustained economic growth to continue, Russia must generate other world-competitive industries. In the long run, the biggest threat to Russia is its inability to compete industrially with the rest of the world. The generation of Russian workers and managers, who were raised under the Communist system, has shown that it has some difficulty in adjusting to the incorporation of new technology and the need for increased productivity in the industrial process. Russia's greatest hope lies with the younger generation to guide the country into a period of more orderly and sustained progress.

Russia's population, like those throughout Eastern Europe, is decreasing sharply. By 2050, its population is projected to decrease to 110 million from 146 million in 2000. This drop represents about one quarter of the population. The decrease in population will change Russia's world population ranking from sixth place in 2000 to fifteenth place in 2050. Starting in 2010, its 20-64 working age group will start decreasing at about a rate of one quarter of a percentage point per year as the 65+ age group increases at about the same rate. The 0-19 youth age group will remain fairly steady, at around 20 percent of the population, during this same period. If this trend is not reversed, a greater financial burden will be placed on fewer working Russians in order to support a larger number of elderly citizens. In addition, Russia also may have to import labor in the future, most likely from the former Soviet republics, in order to sustain its projected economic growth of around 5 percent per year.

Economic strength is vital to Russia if it is to remain a major power in the world. In terms of the GDP, Russia ranks tenth in the world with $1.4 trillion in 2004, in comparison with the first ranked United States, which had a GDP of $11.75 trillion and second-ranked China, which had a GDP of $7.3 trillion. Russia's 2004 per capita GDP of $9,800 is relatively low, placing it in the neighborhood of developing countries such as Mexico, Malaysia, and South Africa. Russia has a wide natural resource base, including major deposits of oil, natural gas, coal, and many strategic minerals. It ranks number one and two, respectively, in the world in output of gas and oil products. However, it lags behind other industrial nations substantially in production of machinery, motor vehicles, and electronics. Russia ranks only tenth in terms of motor vehicle output. Thus, Russia's economy is divided into two parts: a profitable, internationally integrated energy sector and a much larger, insulated, low productivity old-style sector. This second sector puts a damper on Russia's overall economic growth. In addition, as Russia has transformed itself into a market economy, about two thirds of Russian industry has become privatized. These companies are now owned by government and industry insiders who were able to use their positions to translate administrative control into personal possession. In the process, considerable personal fortunes were made. Consequently, many Russian enterprises are dominated by managers who are very suspicious of outside investors or even bank creditors, as they believe they will limit their own power. Investment, structural change, and growth suffer as a result. Economic theory suggests that insider-dominated economies are problematic because they often do not lead to the economic growth and robustness that are connected with market economies that are the result of a more equitable distribution of property rights. Thus, structural reforms are needed to overhaul the financial sector and broaden investment in order to provide for continued economic growth.

The current government is trying to address some of the socio-economic problems that cloud Russia's economic future. Some key economic legislation has been enacted. Russia has met its debt obligations, and it has gone on to amass a post- Soviet era high in reserves, which are expected to be $150 billion by end of 2005. Nonetheless, it lags far behind the West in the wealth possessed by its corporations, institutions, and private citizenry.

Russia has also reinvigorated military reforms, and has chosen a leaner, better-equipped conventional military force over strategic forces. At first glance, it would appear that Russia has formidable military strength. With about 1 million men under arms, another 2 million in reserve, over 20,000 heavy tanks, 6,300 airplanes, 2,700 helicopters, over 100 warships, 756 ICBMs (3,800 warheads), 348 SLBM delivery systems (2,272 SLBMs), and 69 bombers (788 warheads), it appears to be not far behind the U.S. However, this data does not reflect the higher capability of U.S. weaponry. A great many of Russia's military assets are not currently war ready. Nonetheless, Russia still possesses a formidable nuclear deterrent force. Recent reports from Russia indicate the development of a "unique" new generation of nuclear weapons that are capable of overcoming United States's planned missile defense system which is currently in the research and development phase. Russia's military budget of about $65 billion[3] in 2005, while only one-seventh of the U.S. defense budget, still ranks second in the world.

On the international front, Russia is attempting to improve relations with the West, particularly the United States. To promote its power identity, Russia has sought to focus its cooperation with the United States on issues that would emphasize Russia's capacity to be on equal terms with the leading world power. Thus, Russia's foreign policy initiatives center on bilateral cooperation, arms control, nonproliferation of weapons of mass destruction, and fight against terrorism. However, a number of other issues, which include NATO's expansion eastward, U.S. development of an anti-missile defense system, Russia's hard-line policy in Chechnya, and U.S. criticism of Russia's political restructuring, continue to cloud U.S./Russia relations. Until Russia feels stronger, both economically and militarily,

---

[3] The officially announced figure is lower, but actual defense spending more likely is about $65 billion.

it intends to avoid a major confrontation with the U.S. On the other hand, Russia's relations with Western Europe have steadily improved, as, especially, France, Germany, and Spain have strived to integrate Russia into the mainstream of Europe.

Currently, efforts are underway to conclude a Russia-EU agreement which would focus on cooperation in four key areas: the economy, external security, justice matters, and cultural affairs. In Chechnya, where Russia has been fighting Chechen separatists for over a decade, a referendum held in March 2003 approved a new regional constitution, making Chechnya a separatist republic within Russia. Nonetheless, terrorist attacks have continued and, occasionally, have spilled over to neighboring regions, as the Chechnya problem appears to defy a solution by force. Recently, Russia suffered political setbacks in two of its former republics, as, in bloodless revolutions, pro-Western governments were brought to power in Georgia (in November 2003) and Ukraine (in December 2004). As a result, the Commonwealth of Independent States (CIS), established in 1991 to coordinate the foreign and economic policies of the former Soviet republics (considered by Russia to be its sphere of influence), lost some of its effectiveness. Most members remain wary of Russia's power and possible domination. Russia's relations with the major countries of the East, namely China, Japan, and India, have been relatively smooth. These relations are expected to get an additional boost when the planned oil pipeline linking Russia, China, and Japan is completed by the end of the decade.

Russia's major economic strength is the energy sector, which it could use to gain leverage in its foreign relations with other countries. In addition, as an independent, non-OPEC oil producer, with a production level of about 10 million barrels per day (mbpd) in 2005 (out of a total world production of 90 mbpd), Russia has the ability to affect the price of oil worldwide if it would be to its political advantage. Because the government has considerable control over the energy sector, the ability of Russia to affect the price of oil is of some concern to the West, especially the U.S.

By virtue of its location, Russia is concerned with both the East and the West. To the West, Russia has greatly improved relations with Europe. In the short term, Russia needs Europe to accept its new status, expand trade and investment opportunities, and become a customer for its energy supplies. In the long term, Russia sees Europe as a partner in counterbalancing a powerful and unilaterally-acting U.S. Europe, as a whole, has not yet fully embraced Russia as a close partner, even though relations with France and Germany have improved considerably. It will take some time for the whole of Europe to warm up to Russia. East European countries in particular were dominated by Russia under the Communist rule, and they are very determined not to come under Russian rule again.

In addition, Europe's institutional arrangements (NATO, EU) prevent it from establishing closer ties with Russia. Nonetheless, Europe may be drawn much closer to Russia in the future, as European nations become increasingly dependent on Russian energy supplies. To the East, Russia's relations with Asian heavyweights China and India are friendly because of mutual interests. Both China and India need Russia for arms supplies and as a counterbalance to the U.S.

While Russia is still in a weakened position relative to its Soviet Union period, it continues to play an important role in world affairs. This is because of its strategic location between Europe and Asia, its opposition to U.S. unilateralism, which is shared by both China and some European nations, and its rich energy resources, which are needed by Europe, China and Japan.

It should be noted that Russia has made a remarkable recovery from the days when the Soviet Union collapsed, and its resurgence may not be temporary.

ISLAMIC BELT

The Islamic Belt consists of a string of countries with a Moslem majority in their populations. It extends from Northwestern Africa to Southeast Asia centered on 30° latitude. Islam, the Arabic word for submission (to God), has its origins in the preaching of Mohammed on the Saudi-Arabian peninsula in the 600's AD, and it was subsequently spread by Arab conquests throughout North Africa, the Middle and Near East and some parts of Central and Eastern Asia. Currently, the governments of the countries that make up the Islamic Belt have different forms of government, which include: multiparty, republican, military, monarchical, and Islamic. However, even the ones that have representative governments do not fully meet the standards of Western democracies. What most of these countries have in common is political and social instability, which leads to frequent changes in governments often through revolt, coupe, or assassinations. The underlying cause of this volatility is a rapidly growing population, high unemployment rates and governments which mostly cater to elites that keep them in power at the expense of the frustrated masses. Militancy among the disproportionately young population (in most Islamic Belt countries the 15-29 age group makes up nearly 30 percent of the population) is often directed at the West, as, they are seen as the former colonial masters and supporters of their often corrupt and oppressive governments. The U.S., as the leader of the West and supporter of the Moslem despised state of Israel, is frequently singled out.

Today, much of the world's attention is focused on the oil producing regions of the Islamic Belt. Saudi Arabia, Iraq, and Iran alone possess about three quarters of the world's known oil reserves. The United States sees these countries as being of great interest to U.S. national security because of their vast oil reserves, and their geographic location, which provides a gateway to Southern Russia and China. The invasion of Iraq was part of the strategy to secure control over the remaining world's oil resources and to extend U.S. influence in the easterly direction along the Islamic Belt toward both Russia and China. An important element of this strategy is the desire to make the region more secure for the State of Israel which is considered a key ally in the region with close, unquestionable allegiance to the U.S. Currently, U.S. policy is to apply diplomatic and political pressure to those Arab governments that do not accept Israel's right to exist in the region, and to reward those who show a receptive attitude toward Israel.

The fast growing populations of the Arab countries that border Israel create a problematic situation for Israel's security. In 2005, the populations of Arab countries bordering Israel totaled 100 million, as compared to Israel's 6 million, 22 percent of which are Israeli Arabs. The large population of Arabs living on lands surrounding Israel will continue to pose a serious security problem for Israel, despite its large advantage in modern weaponry, which includes a nuclear arsenal. This disparity in Arab/Israeli population size will only increase in the future, as the populations of Arab countries that surround Israel grow at a rate that is 25 percent faster than the growth rate of the population of Israel.

The vast majority of the Islamic Belt countries are best classified as developing countries. For the most part, they lack solid industrial bases and generally have limited access to technology. Furthermore, relatively low literacy rates (most are below 75 percent) make it difficult for them to compete with industrially developed nations. Only the countries with large supplies of desirable natural resources can sustain growing economies through export of these commodities. Those lacking oil and gas have weak economies that are marked by high unemployment and inflation rates which result in poverty of the masses. Throughout the I-Belt, a great divide exists between a small minority of rich and a vast majority of poor which make these countries a likely breeding ground for terrorists. Most of the terrorist threat is directed at the West, particularly the U.S., which is perceived as an infringer on their sovereignty, exploiter of their resources, and bitter enemy of their culture. The U.S.'s unequivocal support of Israel is frequently offered as proof of a hostile attitude towards all Moslems. This conviction is espoused not only by the poor, but by the elite and some leaders of the Islamic Belt countries. Many of them sympathize with the terrorists and consider them freedom fighters or holy warriors.

The military capabilities of the Islamic Belt countries vary considerably. The larger of these countries, namely Pakistan, Turkey, Iran, and Egypt, maintain large armed forces; however, their training, motivation, and effectiveness are questionable. Only a small portion of their weaponry can be considered top of the line by Western standards. The most significant capability is that of Pakistan which has a number of atomic bombs and warheads, with the means to deliver them at long ranges via airplanes and missiles. Turkey, as a member of NATO, has the largest and most capable inventory of tanks, airplanes, and warships, as well as superior capabilities in communications, logistics, and training. Egypt's capabilities appear formidable on paper; yet, their training, logistics, and communications are questionable. Iran's armed forces, while smaller and not as well trained as Turkey's, have considerable self-developed, long-range missile capabilities for the delivery of conventional warheads at ranges in excess of 900 miles, which puts much of the Middle East in their range. Iran also has a nuclear program, which it claims is peaceful and will be used only to generate electricity. The U.S., however, claims that Iran is trying to build atomic bombs and has put mounting pressure on Iran to terminate its nuclear program. If Iran resists U.S. pressure and develops atomic weapons, the security situation in the Greater Near East region will change dramatically. A preemptive strike on Iran's nuclear facilities by the U.S. or joint U.S./Israeli forces cannot be ruled out in view of the importance of this matter to the national security of both countries.

Despite frequent criticism of U.S. Middle East policies, most governments along the Islamic Belt value their relationships with the U.S. Visits to Washington by heads of State and warm reception of them by U.S. Presidents show the population in the Middle East that they command respect in the West and have influence over U.S. policy in the region. Frequently, agreements reached with the U.S. are not reported publicly, since they are not always in line with expectations of the people back home. The I-Belt countries have frequent disagreements amongst themselves as to how to deal with the West, on policies toward Israel, and on relations between themselves. Frequently, meetings of regional leaders result in either no resolution of the region's problems or, less often, in disputes. At times, conflicts develop between them as in the case of the Iraq/Iran war in the 1980's.

The Islamic Belt countries have relatively good relations with the East, mainly because they are not immediately threatened by them. They also see the East as a counterbalance to the West and their policies.

The Islamic countries are neither pro-East nor pro-West. They have their own agenda to build, in the long-term, an Islamic world. No outsider can fully transform the Islamic Belt, as it has to transform itself to produce lasting results. Currently, the Islamic masses are sustained by their religion, and consequently, devoted to it. Only a measure of social and economic equality with the developed world could produce a climate favorable to a transformation that would lead to a separation of state and religion in the Islamic world.

Hard Going in the West

Following the successful Persian Gulf War (Operation Desert Storm) in February 1991, and the formal declaration of the end of the Cold War at the Bush/Yeltsin meeting at Camp David in February 1992, the United States was accepted throughout the globe as the world's only superpower. The Gulf campaign assembled a UN-authorized coalition force that included troops from the U.S., U.K., France, Egypt, and even Syria, among others, under the command of U.S. General Norman Schwarzkopf. The objective was pure and simple: to liberate Kuwait from the Iraqi invasion. This joint, multi-nation effort was heralded by the international community as an example of how world order could be maintained in the future. Civilian causalities were relatively low because Kuwait was liberated in less than a week, and most of the combat took place in the sparsely populated Kuwaiti and Iraqi deserts. Fearing a prolonged period of chaos and a regime change favoring Iran, the U.S. stopped short of marching on Baghdad to oust Saddam Hussein, and the war ended in an armistice agreement. UN Security Council imposed sanctions prior to the war, which barred Iraq from selling oil exports except in exchange for food and medicine, remained in effect. In 1991 and 1992, no-fly zones to protect Shiites and Kurds were established by the UN and enforced by U.S. and U.K. aircraft. The U.S. effort to seek international consensus for the war was universally applauded.

During the early 1990's, the West appeared solidly unified through NATO and the European Union. The extension of both was planned in order to include Eastern European countries. The United States's position as the leader of the West and the world's only superpower remained unchallenged. As the leading industrial and military power in the world, the U.S.'s power was unmatched.

Despite the apparently secure position of the U.S. in the world, the bombing of the World Trade Center in February 1993, the attacks on U.S. embassies in Kenya and Tanzania in August 1998, and the bombing of the USS Cole in October 2000 propelled to the forefront a new threat, that of terrorism. Islamic terrorists, who opposed U.S. policies, culture, and perceived arrogance, discovered a weakness that the U.S. could not defend against with tanks, airplanes, or missiles. While the threat of terrorism is a global problem, the U.S., as the leader of the West and primary perpetrator of injustice on the Islamic world, is seen as the main target.

In the mid-1990's, concern over a world dominated by a single country began to be voiced by leaders of some countries predominantly those of Russia, China, and the I-Belt countries. The dangers of American hegemony were vigorously debated in the foreign press. Even some of the

U.S.'s Western allies started to show some concern. France and Germany began to promote the European Union as a potentially healthy balance to a powerful U.S. The prospect of a strong European Union with its own joint defense capabilities and rapid reaction forces that could protect European interests in regional conflicts appealed to some European countries. Some other nations decided they would take a wait and see attitude. Still, others took the United States's position which was that the plan to develop independent EU planning and defense capabilities would duplicate NATO, which could potentially put NATO's long-term necessity into question. During the Cold War, NATO's primary goal was to protect its members from the Soviet threat; however, this purpose became obsolete when the Soviet Union dissolved. Nonetheless, U.S. national interests, which were projected on the basis of potential future needs due to a possible resurgent Russia, and a growing threat from China, dictated that NATO remain fully in control of military and policy matters. This left the EU as a mere participant in a larger U.S. scheme. Although compromises were made to provisionally satisfy both parties, in the long run, this major policy issue remains unresolved. This issue has only deepened as more countries, particularly those in Eastern Europe, joined both NATO and EU. If NATO has the upper hand in Europe, then the U.S., through its leadership role in NATO, wins the overall military and policy control for most of Europe, all the way to the borders of Russia. However, should the French/German position of a strengthened and independent EU prevail, NATO's future position may become ambiguous. This tug-of-war between the divergent positions of U.S. and EU continue to be an irritant between the Western allies, and this issue has the potential to cause a major rift in their alliance in the future.

The people of Europe are becoming more conservative as demographics change. These changes will eventually result in a much older population. The young segment of the population, those in the 0-19 age group, is decreasing and the 65+ age group has started to grow at unprecedented rates. The new population mix, on the whole, rejects hegemony, militarism, and unilateralism. EU's more conciliatory stance in foreign affairs is a more accurate reflection of the temperament of this increasingly influential population sector. NATO is considered a relic of the Cold War. In time, it is likely that there will be a backlash against European leaders who continue to pursue foreign policies, for either political or economic reasons, that support military solutions in lieu of negotiated settlements. This could result in their eventual removal through the election process. Politicians who support large defense budgets may be in the same predicament. Circumventing the UN, as the U.S. did in the 2003 war on Iraq, is considered by Europeans to be unacceptable, and they will expect their governments to decline to support such actions.

In the Kosovo Conflict (1998-1999), a NATO force, without the UN's official blessing (it was vetoed by Russia and China in the Security Council) drove the Serbian army out of Kosovo. The U.K. was again squarely beside the U.S. both on the ground and in the air. Other allies, including Italy and Germany, provided facilities and logistical assistance, but at the end of the war, the majority of people in these two countries did not believe that this was necessarily the best way to solve the Balkan crisis. The destruction of cities caused by relentless bombing, civilian casualties, and masses of miserable refugees, less than 250 miles from their borders, did not sit well with the Italians and Germans.

After the 9-11 terrorist attack, the world rallied to support the U.S., even Russia was on the U.S. side. When it became clear that, despite a U.S. ultimatum, Afghanistan's Taliban would not cooperate with the United States, the U.S., with the support of Northern Afghans attacked Afghanistan in October 2001. A relentless bombing campaign followed. This campaign eventually defeated the Taliban, and it drove some of the remaining loyalists underground and across the border of Pakistan. Civilians were the main victims, as they had been in previous conflicts. Four years after the end of the war, the Afghan government is still not totally in control of the country.

In Afghanistan, both drug cultivation and trafficking, as well as corruption, continue. A 2004 election installed U.S. protégé Hamid Karzai as the first elected President of the country, but the government's control outside the capital and its surrounding area is limited. Peacekeepers, who were reluctantly contributed by NATO members, are balancing a delicate peace. A U.S. force of 18,000 troops is primarily confined to bases. Occasionally, missions to search for and destroy remnants of the Taliban and al-Quaeda are carried out with marginally successful results. Mullah Muhammad Omar, the Taliban leader, and Osama bin Laden are still at large and in hiding. Security is poor, and frequently, attacks occur even in areas that are under government control. A push by NATO forces to establish its presence in West Afghanistan has been delayed several times as they await additional troop contributions from member countries. No significant reconstruction has taken place, and foreign investments have been very limited because of the lack of security.

In 2002, only three years after Kosovo and one year after the conflict in Afghanistan, the U.S. again went to war. The pre-war scenario, created by the U.S. government, was tailored to the Iraqi regime in power, and had a now familiar content. It goes like this: an evil regime headed by a brutal leader is in possession of weapons of mass destruction that threaten the peace of the whole region, and the leader needs to be eliminated and replaced with a democratic government. An ultimatum was issued to Saddam Hussein insisting that he relinquish the weapons of mass destruction. It was not met, and the war began. A period of sustained bombing was followed by a land invasion of Iraq by troops from the U.S. and the U.K. The Iraqi army was defeated in less than three weeks. Heavy civilian causalities were inflicted, despite claims of accurate bombs based on new technologies. France and Germany, two key Western European allies, balked at participating in this action, which was only peripherally connected to the fight against terrorism. Moreover, they saw this as designed by the U.S. in order to change the prospects of the Middle East to better fit American national interests in the region. Out of all the important Western European allies, only the U.K., Italy, and Spain joined the U.S. The Spanish government that had supported the war was voted out of office in 2004, and subsequently, Spain withdrew its troops from Iraq. Russia joined France and Germany in opposing the war, which was not formally approved by the UN. China also opposed the war primarily on the principle of sovereignty. Furthermore, U.S. relations with Turkey were strained, as it would not allow its territory to be used as a staging area for the war.

As in Afghanistan, the war ended with a victory for the coalition forces, but the insurgency against them continues. Following the script used in

Afghanistan, a U.S. backed interim government was installed, and a coalition force consisting of U.S. troops, and those contributed by supportive countries, was assembled to provide security and for peacekeeping operations. An Iraqi police force and a National Guard were formed with the intention that they will eventually take over these responsibilities when their training is completed. The U.S. again solicited contributions for the reconstruction of Iraq, but, as in the case of Afghanistan, the pledges did not meet the requirements by a wide margin. Reconstruction was slow, as money that had been budgeted for reconstruction could not be spent due to poor security. The oil was again flowing, but below pre-war levels. Chaos, violence, and unemployment continue. Elections were held in January, 2005 for an assembly to form the government and write the Constitution. The Shiite Alliance party, with alleged ties to Iran, received the majority of the votes. However, despite the elections and the formation of a new government headed by Prime Minister Ibrahim al-Jaafari, violence and maneuvering by various ethnic factions to gain power continues. As the insurgency has intensified, some governments have begun to examine the root causes of terrorism. Many in the Islamic Belt countries are convinced that the war against terrorism is, in reality, a fight against Moslems. In the United States, the war has received mixed support. The removal of Saddam has been considered positive. However, the unilateral method that the U.S. used to accomplish it has not been considered wise, and has been met with considerable disapproval.

The combination of U.S. unilateralism and the United States's failure to recognize Europe's concerns, has aroused an anti-American feeling against U.S. policies in Europe. The American position interprets Europe's hesitation to fully support the U.S. as ungratefulness. A rift, as small as it might be, is beginning to develop between them. In many ways, American policy is turning Europe away from supporting the United States position. In the fight against terrorism, the U.S. is also pressuring its traditional allies in the Moslem world to institute more democratic reforms. However, the Islamic world, despite negative media coverage due to accusations of sponsoring terrorism, is becoming more belligerent. Islamic nationalists are fast becoming Islamic militants as they resist the imposition on them of Western ideas and institutions incompatible with their culture, traditions, and religion. The people of the I-Belt countries expect their governments to resist any attempts to use the fight against terrorism as a vehicle to encroach on their sovereignty. As emphasis on full sovereignty and demands for a just resolution of the Israel/Palestine conflict are coming to the forefront, Western oil interests in the Islamic world could be adversely affected if progress on these issues is not made. Increased oil production by I-Belt countries, to lower world oil prices to satisfy the West, could be a thing of the past. The poor opinion of the United States by the Moslem world reflects on the West as a whole and makes it difficult for the West to persuade governments of this region to adopt meaningful reforms.

The tendency to refer to the U.S. as the sole superpower is declining as the world opinion on U.S. foreign policy becomes more negative and its vulnerability to terrorism becomes more apparent. Should the U.S. decide to invade Iran, even fewer countries would support the American effort. Furthermore, the world is beginning to question American integrity, as a number of allegations, including that of presence of WMDs in Iraq, have proven false. Placing the blame on poor intelligence is not fully accepted.

Additionally, revelations of Iraqi prisoner abuse have disgusted the world and further angered the Moslems.

Some Western countries have decided to bring their troops home, while others have remained in the coalition. Suddenly, the unity of the West, that remained so strong during the Cold War, appears to be cracking. As insurgency persists in Afghanistan and Iraq with no clear end in sight, the West also faces growing economic challenges that are intensified by the cost of the Iraq/Afghanistan wars, homeland security against terrorism, and higher oil prices. Furthermore, the social security costs associated with aging populations are on the horizon. To a great extent, the financial burden of Iraq and Afghanistan has fallen on the U.S. The costs to the U.S. for military operations and reconstruction in Iraq and Afghanistan will amount to nearly $300 billion by the middle of 2006. The homeland security budget is, on average, about $10 billion annually. Comparatively, the European contribution has been relatively low.

Higher oil prices have increased further the U.S. trade deficit, and some fear inflationary pressure if the trend continues. The looming cost of increased health care and social security for a growing aged population in both Europe and the U.S. are also pressing issues. In the U.S., large budget deficits are projected. In general, the economic growth in the West has been moderate at best since 2000. As the events of the last five years indicate, the peaceful prosperity expected by the West for the post-Cold War era did not fully materialize after a promising beginning in the 1990's.. Terrorism is a major global problem and conflicts continue to erupt frequently. NATO's role in Europe is waning, as U.S. and Western Europe have different national interests and divergent views on maintaining world order. There are increasing doubts in Western Europe about the motives behind the U.S. led war on terrorism. Additionally, a growing percentage of Europeans want foreign policy and security arrangements to be independent from the U.S. The animosity of the Islamic Belt countries towards the U.S. has grown considerably. In sum, the powerful position of the U.S., after the breakup of the Soviet Union, has eroded significantly when it is compared to China or Russia. The United States's status as the only superpower is questionable.

EAST ON THE MARCH

Since the end of the war in Vietnam in 1975, the East Asia/Pacific region has been relatively free of major conflicts. Most countries in this region have concentrated on improving their economies and the standard of living.

Japan, with the help of the U.S., was the first to develop a world-class economy. By the late 1970's, Japan had become the most industrialized country in Asia, and the second greatest economic power after the United States. Japan became one of the world's leading producers of machinery, motor vehicles, ships, steel, and high-technology goods. Consequently, manufactured goods made up the vast majority of the nation's exports. In recent years, Japan has increasingly shifted some of its industries overseas through outsourcing, and it has made massive capital investments abroad, especially in the U.S. and around the Pacific Rim (including China). Japan has also become a global leader in financial services. Some of the world's largest banks are in Japan. Although the Japanese economy has undergone a period of very low growth or, in some cases stagnation, Japan remains one of the wealthiest countries in the world and certainly the wealthiest in Asia.

Despite great economic wealth, Japan has hesitated, since its defeat in World War II, to take on a more active role in world affairs. Its armed forces, while modern by Asian standards, are defensive in nature. Its population of 127 million is dwarfed by China's 1.3 billion. In addition, Japan's demographic trends are not favorable, as its 20-64 working age group is declining and its 65+ senior age group is sharply increasing.

The balance of power between Japan and China has changed drastically in recent years. Japan has lost some of its economic and international influence over the past decade. China, on the other hand, has become an ascending power with a fast-growing economy and increasing nuclear capabilities. The likelihood of Japan rearming to give its military offensive capabilities is low as it would require a constitutional change and because of Japan's wartime history with China, Korea, and Southeast Asia in general. The more likely scenario would be that, eventually, Japan will accept China's leadership in Asia, and, instead, be content to become the technological center of the region. As the competition between the East and West intensifies, Japan will clearly have to make a choice. For some countries that time has already come, and they have chosen China.

China, while clearly the rising star of the region, has shown considerable patience and moderation in international affairs, as it cautiously but confidently continues on the course to become the leading power of the East. In some ways, China is already there. Although technologically still inferior to Japan, its stature in the past decade has risen sharply, due to its phenomenally rapid economic development, tempered conduct in the international arena, and growing military arsenal.

In a way, China is reaching its peak in an Asian vacuum. Japan is stagnating, India is not yet ready, and the fourth Asian giant, Indonesia, is confronted with separatist movements and is not fully ready to compete with the likes of China.

The U.S.'s military capabilities in this part of the world have remained relatively unchanged since the end of the Vietnam War in 1975. Its forces in Japan, Korea, and Guam are powerful from the air and sea, but no match for the forces of China on the ground. The United States's attempt to use a coalition of its Pacific allies (Japan, South Korea and Australia), as a counterbalance to China, has not been particularly effective due to a lack of historical ties between these countries. In addition, the U.S. is currently preoccupied with trying to force North Korea to end its nuclear program.

By any standards, the growth of the Chinese economy has been remarkable. In the last five years, China's economy grew at an average rate of just under 10 percent per year. Globally, China is generating about 15 percent of the global GDP. Chinese markets have become more open, competitive, and predictable. Imports and exports, meanwhile, are growing faster than at any time in the past five years, due to the regional economic recovery, continued high demand by the U.S., and Western Europe, as well as a growing domestic market. China's total trade in 2004 surpassed $1.1 trillion, which makes China the world's third largest trading nation.

The economic expansion has raised the standard of living for most Chinese, led to rapid urbanization and accelerated improvement of infrastructure. Nevertheless, regional imbalances exist, as the coastal regions of China are developing much more quickly than the central regions, which is once again reminiscent of Britain during the Industrial Revolution. A high rate of unemployment is also a problem. However, China prefers to give economic development the highest priority, and to address the social problems in the development process. The government is concerned that a drive to provide social equity in the labor market, particularly when it involves trade unions, could sacrifice efficiency. Despite social imbalances and some corruption at different levels of the government, in comparison with the past, almost every person living in China is better off.

China's tremendous progress can only be measured appropriately by looking at the past. Now, China has thirty-six cities with a population of more than one million people, which is eight more than just two decades ago. When the People's Republic was founded in 1949, only about 35 airports existed; facilities were so limited that even an aircraft as small as DC-4 could only land in three of the larger cities. Today, there are over 200 civilian airports and aviation is one of the largest growth industries in the country. In 2004, a total of 200 million passengers passed through Chinese airports. Twenty years ago, it was rare for a family to have a telephone. Today, there is an average of 30 telephones per 100 persons nationwide. Ten years ago, most Chinese people had never seen a mobile phone. Today, almost 300 million Chinese people own one. Beijing, Shanghai, and Guangzhou, which were relatively obscure cities 25 years ago, have become major centers for manufacturing and commerce. Four Chinese cities including Beijing, Shanghai, Tianjin, and

Guangzhou now have underground rail transit systems. Two other cities, Nanjing and Shenzhen, are in the process of building them. In 2002, the first commercial levitation train, based on German technology, was put into operation along a 20 mile long stretch between Shanghai's airport and financial district. In 2005, China's $30 billion upgrade to its railway network was completed. China's growing space program put an astronaut into orbit in October 2003, which made it only the third country (after Russia and U.S.) to ever launch a person into space.

China's tremendous potential leads to the conclusion that the economic expansion witnessed so far is just the beginning. China is a hard working nation, with a long history of civilizations. As the most populous country in the world, it can readily supply quality labor at a low cost. Furthermore, the size of the population creates a huge domestic market with tremendous untapped potential. As the economy continues to grow, the per capita income of Chinese workers will continue to increase, which will consequently generate a still larger market for its goods. In addition, China's relatively stable political system and rapidly improving infrastructure provide a strong environment for investment that is favored by international investors. As the Chinese become wealthier, they too will become investors in China. Barring some unexpected calamity, this cycle should continue well into the future.

In the years following the Tiananmen Square incident in June 1989, many countries reduced their diplomatic contacts with China and limited their economic assistance programs. During the period that followed, China vigorously tried to reestablish normal relations. By late 1990, it had succeeded to erase to some degree the memories of Tiananmen Square, and again, establish good relations with other countries.

In the past decade, China's involvement in international affairs can be characterized as cooperative and constructive. Chinese leaders have been regular travelers to all parts of the world, and China has sought a higher profile in the UN through its permanent seat on the United Nations Security Council. China has improved relations with Russia, jointly signing a Treaty of Friendship and Cooperation in July 2001. The two also joined with the Central Asian nations of Kazakhstan, Kyrgyzstan, Tajikistan, and Uzbekistan to establish the Shanghai Cooperation Organization (SCO) in June 2001. The SCO is designed to promote regional stability and to cooperate in fighting terrorism in the region. In 2005, China and India agreed to form a strategic partnership to end a border dispute and increase trade in an agreement which marked a major shift in relations between the Asian giants. China, however, has notably avoided becoming entangled in any strategic alliances or engaging in regional power politics.

Throughout history, China has found its vital interests tied to the Asia-Pacific region. China clearly understands that it can be more influential in this region than anywhere else. While some countries in the region still may not fully trust China, they are also reluctant to see a power vacuum open to a possible Japanese or joint U.S./Japanese hegemony. If China is able to strengthen its influence over the major players in this dynamic part of the world, through regional co-operative efforts such as the Asian-Pacific Economic Cooperation (APEC), it would pave the way for it to become the leader of the East. Thus, to establish good neighborly relations with all regional countries has recently become a basic objective of China's foreign policy. Most notably, China's positive role as an intermediary in the North Korean nuclear crisis has greatly enhanced its stature among the Asian nations and around the world.

The relationship between the U.S. and China has improved gradually following the U.S. bombing of the Chinese embassy in Belgrade in 1999 and the collision of a Chinese F-8 fighter with a U.S. EP-3 reconnaissance aircraft in 2001. Following the September 11, 2001 terrorist attack on the U.S., China offered strong public support for the war on terrorism. In the UN, China voted for the coalition campaign in Afghanistan, but opposed the U.S. / U.K. invasion of Iraq.

China's foreign policy over the last 10 years can be summarized as increasingly more responsible and worthy of a regional power. Its policy decisions are unencumbered by any alliances, and therefore, are for the most part based on the merits of the issue. With regard to Taiwan, China has proclaimed the one-China policy and its parliament enacted a law in 2005 authorizing force to stop Taiwan from pursuing formal independence. China, however, has stopped short of any military intimidation of the island in recent years.

Internally, the government's efforts to promote rule of law are significant and ongoing. The 1994 Administrative Procedure has allowed citizens to sue officials for abuse of authority or malfeasance. The Chinese Constitution and laws provide for fundamental human rights including due process, but in practice, these are sometimes ignored.

The Chinese military is trying to transform itself from a land based power, which is centered on a vast ground force, into a smaller, mobile, high-tech military capable of operations in regional conflicts. China's power projection capability is limited, but it has grown in recent years, and plans are in place to further increase this capability, which currently includes destroyers, modern aircraft, and diesel submarines purchased from Russia. China's nuclear capabilities are also growing. By 2010, China will replace its liquid fuel CSS-4 ICBMs with solid fuel versions having multi-warhead capabilities. By 2007, China could have Land Attack Cruise Missiles (LACMs) for theater war fighting and strategic attack.

Equally important to its accomplishments in the economic and military arenas has been the development of a national sense of unity and pride. Whether it is competition in the perfection of their manufactured products or in the field of athletics, they want to excel and do well for China. It would not be surprising if, in the 2008 Summer Olympics, which are to be held in Beijing, the Chinese athletes win a record number of gold medals in China's Olympic history.

As impressive as China's recent economic success might be, it is not alone in the region. In addition to Japan's industrial and financial engine, which is still running strong after 50 years, there are India and Indonesia. In the not too distant future these nations may be duplicating China's performance. India, with a rapidly growing population of about 1.1 billion, a GDP of $3.3 trillion, and a growth rate of about 6 percent per year, is not far behind. Indonesia's GDP is about $830 billion and is growing at a 5 percent rate per year, which is quite good for fourth place in the region.

In the East, a realization is setting in that China's rapid economic development could lead to a boom for the entire region. The countries of the East increasingly see China as a huge market for their goods and investments. They can imagine an East where Japan provides the technological expertise, Indonesia the natural resources, and China and India the industrial production and markets.

FUTURE DEVELOPMENTS (BEYOND 2005)

In the short term, between 2005 and 2025, the instability and turbulence in the world will accelerate, as new economic and political pressures are placed on the global system. During this period, the early signs of a worldwide economic stagnation will begin to surface. Initially this will occur in the West, as historic demographic changes begin to take place. The long awaited, but feared, peak in world oil production will occur around the middle of this period, which will further stress the system. International relations will become increasingly tense, as the U.S. attempts to further expand its influence along the Islamic Belt and in Eastern Europe, and tries to counter China's growing power in Asia. At least initially, the Greater Near East and North Korea will continue to be the world's foremost trouble spots, as diplomatic solutions fall short of reaching their goals. Additionally, conflicts in other parts of the world will flare up. Terrorism is likely to intensify, as Moslems, finding no solution to their anger and frustration, turn to violence for revenge. The EU and the

U. S. will become more divided over foreign policy issues, as they perceive vital Western interests in a different light. As the West struggles to find common ground, China will continue to grow economically, and will also solidify its position as the leader in Asia. Essentially, the geopolitical system will fragment into blocks, each with its own agenda to gain a politically and economically commanding position in the world.

In the long term, between 2026 and 2100, the world will experience, in synchronization with a historical slowdown in the rate of population growth, a gradual, but marked movement toward a more peaceful world, where diplomatic solutions predominate over conflicts and goodwill among all peoples prevails. The frantic growth of the world's population, which started around 1750, will come to an end around 2075. East and West will reach parity by that time. However, instead of confronting each other for the domination of the world, the two giant blocks will start cooperating for the good of humanity, as the pitched excitement created by years of rapid population growth will begin to subside.

NEAR TERM (2006-2025)

WEST

A major factor in the shaping of the future world will be the numerical size and composition of its population. Even though the overall world population continues to grow, particularly in Africa and Asia, which includes the I-Belt countries, the global rate of population growth has been slowing since 1963. The first major consequence of the deceleration in the population growth rate will be felt in Europe. For the first time in recorded history, with the exception of the periods in the 1300's and 1600's when the bubonic plague killed thousands of people, Europe's population will start declining in 2010, as Western European nations begin to join the decline already started in parts of Eastern Europe in the early 1990's. The early stages of the population decline almost will be the reverse of what transpired before the start of the Industrial Revolution. Just as the acceleration of population growth then brought on the boom period of industrial expansion, a reversal of that trend will bring on industrial retrenchment in modern Europe. Excess industrial capacity will begin to surface and economic growth will stagnate as the consumer base slowly shrinks to new lows. Industrial retrenchment will also result in worker layoffs and chronic unemployment. The building industry will slump, and educational facilities will be scaled down as student enrollment declines. The rest of the world, with the exception of Japan, which is going to experience a similar population decline to Europe's, will remain, as yet, unaffected directly. However, reduced European imports will have a significant impact on their economies. U.S. exports to Europe totaled about $170 billion in 2004 and were the largest of any country in the world; resultantly, Europe's population decline will negatively impact the U.S. economy.

The West's aging population will be an additional demographic shift that will have a negative impact. Beginning around 2010, the populations of U.S., Canada, and Europe will begin to experience a sharp increase in the 65+ age group. By 2025, 20-25 percent of their populations will be 65 or older. By contrast, in the East this age group will remain mostly below the 15 percent mark. The notable exception will be Japan, with 28 percent of its population being over 65. The West's aging populations will be an additional burden on their economies, as the 65+ age group historically contributes about 30 percent less to consumer spending and GDP growth than the rest of the population, but this older group requires greater government budgetary resources to pay for their pensions and health benefits. As the costs of these benefits increase, they will become one of the highest expenditures for the U.S. and Western Europe. Progress in all areas will be impeded, as an aged society tends to be more conservative and less innovative. In addition, as growth of Western economies slows, the price of oil, an important factor in the cost of doing business, will increase as world oil production peaks around 2015, at about 40 billion barrels of oil per year. The U.S. and Western Europe will be affected the most, as they depend heavily on oil for industry and transportation. When oil production peaks, they will consume about 40 percent of world's oil. By 2015, only a few countries, namely Saudi Arabia, Iraq, Iran, Kuwait, United Arab Emirates, and Russia will, in any significant quantity export oil. However, the demand for oil will be much higher because many developing countries, particularly China and India, will increase their demand, as they become more industrialized. China's oil consumption, for example, will almost double from 5.4 million barrels per day in 2005 to 8.8 million barrels per day in 2015. China will only produce 3.2 barrels per day on its own in 2015 which will create a shortfall of 5.6 million barrels daily, all of which will need to be imported. The U.S. will produce 10.4 million barrels per day in 2015, but still will need to import an additional 13.5 million barrels daily to satisfy its consumption needs.

As oil consumption needs grow and become larger than can be produced, shortfalls will develop, and the price of oil will increase sharply. Increasing production from aging fields is expensive, and would only postpone the oil production peak by a few years. Technology to help reduce the shortfall, like cars powered by hydrogen fuel cells, is developing slowly, and the infrastructure to support it requires large investments. At the current pace of development, this technology will not be fully in place by 2015. Alternate energy sources, such as oil extracted from tar sands and shale, are expensive to develop and will raise the price of oil to levels that will cause damaging inflationary trends in the Western economies. The countries with the biggest shortfalls, which include the U.S., Japan, China, Germany, and France, will be in heated competition over the dwindling oil supplies. The U.S. will attempt to control the I-Belt's oil supply to its advantage. Should Islamic governments deny an adequate supply of oil to the U.S., the United States may take control of oil fields in the interest of national security. Europe, Japan, and China will increasingly turn to Russia in order to satisfy their oil and gas energy needs. This will give Russia an advantage in the political arena, as these countries become dependent on it for their energy supplies.

In the West, higher energy costs combined with a shrinking consumer base and increased government spending on an aging population will have a damaging effect on the economies of both the U.S. and Western Europe. U.S. budget deficits will grow, and debt will accumulate. The EU countries, which are limited in the amount of debt they can carry, will further reduce defense spending. The economic pressures could very well result in a prolonged recession in the West. As the world's economic health deteriorates, the world will become more dangerous. Existing security blocks, especially NATO, will diminish in effectiveness, as the strategy to isolate and weaken Russia by establishing a foothold closer to its borders, through extension of NATO's membership to Eastern European countries, will not bring the desired results. These Eastern European countries, as well as the Western European countries, will increasingly be drawn economically closer to Russia as it becomes both their trade partner and main supplier of energy.

As the economic well-being of the countries in the Eastern and Western Europe take precedence over military readiness, the ability of the U.S. to draw on NATO resources in conflicts it initiates in its national interest will diminish significantly. Fewer NATO members will be ready to join coalition forces for combat or for peacekeeping missions. The U.S. will become increasingly isolated in its ability to exert diplomatic or military pressure on Russia, China, or any of the Islamic Belt countries. Even its close and special relationship with the U.K. will be stressed.

Above all, the people of the I-Belt countries will continue to resist Western influence and meddling, as well as Western troops stationed in their territories, regardless of the reason for it. Governments of Moslem countries that allow the presence of Western troops on their soil, will likely face insurgencies and revolts intended to remove them from power.

In Asia, the attempt by the U.S. to form a coalition of Japan, South Korea, and other willing Asian countries to counterbalance China will lose steam as China clearly becomes the dominant power of the region. North Korea, with its small but deadly arsenal of nuclear weapons and the missiles to deliver them, will increasingly pose a more dangerous threat to the U.S. and its interests in the region. However, the U.S. options to effectively deal with this situation, despite its military superiority, will remain limited.

As the short term period draws to a close, the option of limited U.S. isolationism will be hotly debated in government circles. The West's co-existence with a powerful but friendly East will increasingly be considered a better alternative to conflicts.

EAST

During the 2006 to 2025 short term period, the East's population will continue to grow at rates equivalent to, or slightly lower than, the preceding 20 years. The notable exception will be Japan, whose population will start declining in 2007. Aging will not yet be a problem in the region. Except for Japan, in all other countries the 65+ age group will be below 15 percent, considerably lower than the West. Thus, demographic indicators will be favorable to a continued economic expansion in the region.

The economic slowdown experienced in the West during this period will also be experienced in the East, as exports to the Western countries decrease. However, as the per capita incomes in Eastern countries rise, a huge consumer base will develop that will recuperate some of the export losses. Although in the past, exports to the West were a prime factor in the economic growth of the East, a wealthier Asian consumer will become an increasingly key element in the economic expansion of the East. This will partially cushion the East from the economic stagnation in the West. The Eastern consumer base will continue to expand as the region's population grows by almost 50 percent by 2050. Hence, the East's economic growth will slow down, but it will probably avoid a prolonged downturn period. As the cost of oil rises, additional pressures will be put on the Eastern economies. Nonetheless, the relatively low cost of labor in the region will partially offset the increase in oil prices, and the East will likely avoid a lengthy and severe economic recession. However, it is possible that a stronger than expected economic downturn in the West could spill over into the East.

During this period, China will begin to assume a leadership role in the East. Barring a significant overflow of West's economic problems, China's industrial modernization and economic expansion should continue, although at reduced levels. By 2025, China's military capabilities will be far superior to any other country in this region, as it begins to develop its own military industry. During this period, Taiwan will most likely amicably revert to China. China's ascent to its role as the leader of the East will be relatively smooth due to its current policy of non-interference and good neighborly relations with the rest of Asia. China's relationship with Russia will be cordial, as China will continue to heavily depend on Russian energy supplies and military hardware.

As China's military and economic strength grows in the region, the U.S. will have little choice but to accept it. China, in turn, will show no aggression or hostility toward the West. Instead, it will put the emphasis on economic cooperation.

Long-Term (2026-2100)

Upon entering the second quarter of the 21st century, the once strong and united West will begin to show some wear and tear. The U.S. strategy of securing a safe future for itself and its Western allies by using its stature as the only superpower to shape the world, will not have made significant progress. Political and economic pressures at home and overseas, will make it increasingly difficult for the U.S. to address multiple fronts successfully. The aging populations in the West will be inclined to favor peaceful resolution of conflicts. The majority of people in the U.S. will prefer a form of limited isolationism, which will strengthen diplomatic and economic cooperation with other countries of the world, but limit the military adventurism used to achieve goals. The well-being of all people, including the aged, will be their priority. This trend will continue as the ethnic mix of the U.S. population undergoes some major changes. The Hispanic and Asian segments of the U.S. population are growing more rapidly than other races, which will result in a changed make-up of the U.S. population. By the year 2060, only 50 percent of the U.S. population will be white (non-Hispanic), 27 percent of the population will be of Hispanic origin, about 10 percent Asian, and 13 percent black. By 2100, the Hispanic origin and Asian parts of the population will be 40 percent and 13 percent, respectively. The perspective of the new population mix will be different, as they see the world as one big melting pot of different nationalities and cultures. They will be less inclined to impose the American way of life on others. Their preferences will be for closer relations with South America and Asia, and they will make it known at the polls.

By 2075, the East will have reached parity with the West economically and militarily. The industrial growth of the East will be broad as India, Indonesia, Malaysia, Thailand, and others join China in achieving high economic and industrial growth on a sustained basis. South Korea and Japan, already highly industrialized, will join to form a formidable Eastern economic block.

The West's military superiority will be negated by the possession of formidable nuclear deterrents by its potential adversaries, namely Russia and China. Conventional warfare, which would put a smaller U.S. force against enemies with much larger armies, will not be an option. As the characteristics of the U.S. population mix change, the key objective of its people will be to strive for peace in the world. The notion of invading another country to change its regime will evoke a sense of wrongdoing among the New Americans.

As the stalemate between the East and West continues, the world population will reach a peak of about 10 billion people around 2075. It will stabilize itself for a short period, and then start to decline modestly. By 2100, it will be down to 9.8 billion. The period that follows the population growth peak will be characterized by industrial retrenchment, as fewer goods are needed to satisfy a shrinking world population. The economic downturn will be world-wide, as industrial capacity is reduced to adjust to the lower demand for goods. Despite the sharp economic downturn and the accompanying hardships it will create, the deceleration in the population growth will have a calming effect on the world. The frenzied competition started in 1750 with the industrialization of the West, and which repeated itself 250 years later in the East, will begin to wane in concert with the marked decline in the world's population and economic growth. The competitive and aggressive environment that was created by the years of rapid population growth will, instead, be replaced by one characterized by calmness and cooperation.

Political tensions will decline, and solutions to world's pressing problems, long neglected during the turbulent era stretching 325 years from about 1750 to 2075, will begin to be addressed. Overcoming the economic downturn caused by the industrial retrenchment, developing alternate energy sources, exploring the depths of the Universe, protecting the environment, and improving the standard of living of the Earth's people everywhere will top the new agenda. Cooperation between East and West will be particularly intense in order to alleviate the consequences of the industrial retrenchment that followed the reversal of population growth around 2075.

Peaceful and tranquil years will follow as both East and West jointly strive to develop a better world. Militarism will be a phenomenon of the past. In this new world, competition will be replaced by cooperation. For the first time in history, the merits of a "world without borders" will be debated in the capitals of the world.

Progress will be slowed, as man's labor will be accomplished in a more relaxed world. The frantic drive to outperform each other fueled by the rapid population growth will disappear. Thus, for the first time since the development of nuclear weapons, the world will be able to relax knowing that the Earth's civilization will not be wiped out by human error or folly.

SOURCES

www.census.gov

www.eia.doe.gov

www.state.gov

www.worldbank.org

www.cia.gov

www.un.gov

www.cdi.gov

www.iiss.org

www.fas.org

Microsoft Encarta Encyclopedia Standard 2005

About The Author

The author has worked as an electronics engineer for the U.S. Navy in the field of Anti-Submarine Warfare (ASW) for forty years (1957-1997). As Head of the Intelligence Branch of the Naval Applied Science Laboratory in New York City, he had responsibility for the development of intelligence systems related to the Navy's ASW programs. Later in his career, the author worked as the Head of the Sonar Development Branch at the Naval Underwater Systems Center in New London, Connecticut and the Naval Undersea Warfare Center in Newport, Rhode Island. His responsibilities included the conduct of programs in the areas of submarine sonar and ocean surveillance.

During his career, the author participated on numerous Navy panels and committees related to acoustic intelligence and sonar systems. In addition, he provided consultations and recommendations on intelligence and technical matters to the Chief of Naval Operations and Naval Sea Systems Command in Washington D.C.

The author was born in Lvov, Ukraine in 1934. In his youth, he attended schools in the Ukraine, Poland, Czechoslovakia, and Austria. In 1949, he immigrated with his parents to the United States. The author graduated from the City College of New York with a Bachelors of Mechanical Engineering degree in 1957 and received a Masters of Public Administration degree from the University of Northern Colorado in 1976.

The author has traveled widely in Europe, South America, and Canada. His personal interests are in the areas of world history and world affairs, and he has read numerous books on these subjects.